T2-CSE-088

DATE RAPE

Other books in the At Issue series:

DATE RAPE

James Haley, *Book Editor*

Daniel Leone, *President*
Bonnie Szumski, *Publisher*
Scott Barbour, *Managing Editor*
Helen Cothran, *Senior Editor*

San Diego • Detroit • New York • San Francisco • Cleveland
New Haven, Conn. • Waterville, Maine • London • Munich

THOMSON

──────✳──────™

GALE

LIBRARY OF CONGRESS CATALOGING-IN-PUBLICATION DATA

Date rape / James Haley, book editor.
  p. cm. — (At issue)
Includes bibliographical references and index.
ISBN 0-7377-1570-7 (pbk. : alk. paper) — ISBN 0-7377-1569-3 (lib. : alk. paper)
  1. Date rape—United States. I. Haley, James, 1968– . II. At issue (San Diego, Calif.)
HV6561 .D36 2003
362.883—dc21
                                                                    2002192799

Printed in the United States of America

Contents

Introduction

In the spring of 1991, a thirty-year-old single mother accused William Kennedy Smith, a nephew of Senator Edward Kennedy and a scion of America's most famous political family, of raping her. The woman had met the thirty-one-year-old Smith, who was enjoying a brief vacation from medical school, at a nightclub in Palm Springs, Florida, not far from the Kennedy's multimillion-dollar estate. After the two left the club together, Smith drove the woman back to the family compound, where he allegedly raped her on the lawn. In December 1991, millions of Americans watched Smith's ten-day trial on television. The complainant tearfully delivered her testimony, describing how an innocent meeting at a nightclub had ended in sexual assault. Smith countered by explaining that the sex was consensual, and, after spending an estimated $1 million in legal fees for his defense, was acquitted of the charges.

Widespread media coverage of Smith's arrest and trial focused national attention on the issue of *date rape*, which is a rape committed by a person with some level of romantic relationship to the victim. *Acquaintance rape* is perpetrated by someone who is not a complete stranger. The allegations against Smith follow a pattern typical of many date/acquaintance rapes, in which a man meets a woman in a public place, gains her confidence, and invites her back to his home. He then engages in nonconsensual sex with the woman through implied or spoken threats of physical harm, the use of force, or taking advantage of her after she has passed out under the influence of drugs or alcohol.

In 1991, the view that a woman could be "date raped" was a new and controversial way of thinking about rape. Most people had long considered rape to be a violent crime committed by a stranger in a dark alley, not an instance of unwanted sex with an acquaintance. Beginning in the late 1980s, however, feminist activists on college campuses promoted a broader definition of rape that included situations in which women were pressured into having sex against their will or violated while intoxicated. They based their reasoning on the results of a survey of college women conducted by University of Arizona Medical School professor Mary Koss, which was funded by the National Institutes of Health and published in 1987. Koss's study found that 27 percent of college women surveyed had experienced a sexual encounter that met the legal definition of rape or attempted rape. In addition, Koss found that 80 percent of these incidents were committed by someone the victim knew. Most of these rapes went unreported to school authorities because, as Koss maintains, the women had an unclear understanding of the legal definition of rape and tended to blame themselves for the rapes. To Koss and the feminist groups who found these numbers disturbing, many more women were victims of rape than previously understood; thus, the term *date rape* offered women a new way to describe rapes that were far more common but just as psychologically damaging as the stereotypical stranger rape.

The mainstream media initially responded to Koss's conclusions with calls for action and "surprise that such large numbers of female students reported having been victims of assaults matching the legal definition of rape," according to Molly Dragiewicz, a professor of women's studies at George Mason University. But by mid-1991, the high-profile William Kennedy Smith trial had ignited a contentious public debate over date rape and accelerated what some feminists dubbed a cultural "backlash" against anti-rape activists. A few critics familiar with research techniques argued that Koss had greatly exaggerated the number of college rape victims by using an overly broad definition of rape and counting regrettable episodes of sexual miscommunication as rape. Other observers questioned whether a broader definition of rape would do the victims of violent rapes a disservice by trivializing the crime of rape. In May 1991, shortly after sexual battery charges were brought against Smith, the *New York Post* published an editorial expressing this concern. It stated, "What strikes us as dangerous is the elasticity of the term 'rape.' We wonder whether it's now being stretched in a manner that causes the American people to underestimate the gravity of the crime itself." The editorial goes on to make a clear distinction between what it views as real rape—a violent, criminal assault against a woman—and a "sexual encounter, forced or not, [that] has been preceded by a series of consensual activities—drinking, a trip to the man's home, a walk on a deserted beach at three in the morning [references to the Smith case]." The editorial provoked a storm of controversy, but *Newsweek, Time,* and the *New York Times* soon followed the *Post's* lead and ran articles that treated the issue of date rape with greater skepticism.

Since the early 1990s, the date-rape debate has continued on college campuses across the United States where co-ed dormitories, alcohol abuse, and casual sex lead to frequent accusations of sexual assault. A National Institute of Justice survey of 4,446 college women published in 2000 found that "for a campus of 10,000 women, . . . the number of rapes could exceed 350. . . . These figures suggest that rape victimization is a potential problem of large proportion and potential public policy interest." Under pressure from parents, campus activists, and the federal government, college administrators have taken action against the perceived threat of date rape by instituting date-rape prevention programs and policies.

Some of these policies have generated controversy, in particular, the unique procedures that colleges follow when adjudicating charges of date rape on campus. Determining the guilt or innocence of the accused often involves a disciplinary hearing conducted by college administrators. Private colleges are not bound by the U.S. Constitution and can conduct hearings under procedural rules of their own design. With little substantive evidence to go on, settling date-rape accusations frequently comes down to one person's word against another's. Critics contend that many hearings, particularly at private colleges, favor the woman's version of events by making it difficult for the accused to present his side of the story. For example, Columbia University, an elite Ivy League school in New York City, has come under fire from civil liberties groups who assert that its sexual misconduct policy violates the basic rights of the accused. According to libertarian commentator Wendy McElroy, sexual misconduct hearings at Columbia "do not allow a 'defendant' to face his accuser or cross-examine witnesses. . . . Nor is the defendant allowed to have an attorney present during the proceeding. With a maximum of ten days' notice . . . the defendant is expected to prepare a defense on which his academic career might hinge." McElroy illustrates the unfairness of this policy with a worst-case scenario involving a student nearing graduation who is accused of having committed date rape in his freshman year (complainants have five years from the date of the alleged incident to file a complaint) and is "denied every basic right of due process guaranteed by the Constitution."

Schools that have amended their sexual misconduct policies in the interest of fairness have met with equal controversy. After receiving criticism for the expulsion of a student accused of date rape in 1999, including protests from some faculty members, Harvard College implemented a new sexual misconduct policy in 2002. This policy was intended to address the "he said, she said" aspect of date-rape accusations by stipulating that "any student who alleges that another student has committed an act of sexual misconduct . . . must provide 'sufficient independent corroboration' or 'proof' before the College will launch an investigation," according to an editorial by attorneys Wendy J. Murphy and Ellenor J. Honig in the *Harvard Crimson*. The policy has been criticized by women who feel that the university is abdicating its responsibility to protect the rights of female students. Murphy and Honig, opponents of the policy, maintain that determining the truth in sexual misconduct investigations has less to do with examining evidence than having properly trained investigators, interviewers, and judges oversee sexual assault cases. On August 5, 2002, the U.S. Department of Education's Office for Civil Rights announced a formal investigation to determine whether Harvard's policy is in violation of Title IX of the Civil Rights Act of 1972—a law that requires schools to have "prompt and equitable" procedures to resolve accusations of sexual harassment and assault. The resolution of this investigation may significantly impact the way campus sexual misconduct policy is written in the future.

The continuing battle over date rape on college campuses illustrates how the expanded definition of rape first advocated by researcher Mary Koss remains a highly controversial issue in American society. On the one hand, it is clear that the concept of date rape has gained a significant level of cultural acceptance due in large measure to the campus and community activism of the anti-rape movement. In addition, the American legal system has taken the "no means no" slogan of feminists seriously; several state courts have handed down sexual assault convictions in cases where the accused acted without force or threats of violence. On the other hand, in a society that values freedom and personal responsibility, critics remain reluctant to endorse a definition of rape that in their view excuses women for behaving irresponsibly. Observes cultural critic Camille Paglia, "Every woman must take personal responsibility for her sexuality. . . . When she makes a mistake, she must accept the consequences." Whether the concept of date rape offers women a meaningful way to define and combat rape is debated and discussed by the authors in *At Issue: Date Rape*.

1

Date Rape Is a Form of Sexual Violence

Scott Lindquist

Scott Lindquist is a rape prevention specialist and the author of The Date Rape Prevention Book, *from which the following viewpoint is excerpted.*

The majority of rapes are date and acquaintance rapes, in which the victim and the assailant are acquainted on some level. The perpetrator wrongly uses force or the threat of force to have sex with the victim against her will or when the victim is physically or mentally unable to give consent. Women, particularly in the college environment, must not drop their guard around men they think they know; instead, they should learn to identify date rapists by understanding the behaviors typical of sex assailants. Date rape is not just a misunderstanding—it is forcibly obtaining power over another individual through the means of sexual assault.

Rape is a sexual assault in which a person uses his penis or other object to commit vaginal, oral, or anal penetration of a victim, by force or threat of force, against the victim's will, or when the victim is physically and/or mentally unable to give consent.

Date rape is simply a rape that happens between two parties who are dating.

Acquaintance rape is a rape that happens when the victim and perpetrator are acquainted. The majority of rapes are actually acquaintance rapes, because in almost every case, the rapist gets to know the victim at least enough for her to drop her guard. Once she lets him into her confidence and begins to trust him, he strikes.

Refusing to hear "no"

It is important to realize that not every victim of rape has signs of physical abuse. Just because her clothes are not shredded, or her bones aren't broken, doesn't mean she didn't resist or that she wasn't raped. The threat of force is, in many cases, just as intimidating as actual violence for the victim. The rapist has used fear to get control of her.

Even though rape is a life-threatening situation, the victim of acquaintance rape may not perceive it as such. The primary difference between stranger rape and date/acquaintance rape is the relationship between the victim and the rapist. The fact that she supposedly knows the rapist at least superficially, may make it more difficult to identify him as dangerous. This fact also may delude her friends and family into disbelieving her. Even more, knowing him can also dilute a woman's normal self-defense response to her attacker and cause her to hesitate in reporting the crime and seeking help for herself.

Date/acquaintance rape can happen to anyone who goes out on a date with or encounters a man who wants power over her in the form of sex and refuses to take no for an answer. Date/acquaintance rape accounts for 84 percent of all reported rapes, and yet it is estimated that only 5 percent of date/acquaintance rapes are reported.

Is it possible that the most charming guy, who may be the leading quarterback for the high school football team, son of the mayor, president of the senior class, or the "perfect gentleman" who works or lives next door, can also be a rapist? Yes, if the circumstances are right and he thinks he can get away with it.

Knowing [the rapist] can . . . dilute a woman's normal self-defense response to her attacker and cause her to hesitate in reporting the crime.

Reality Check: After you say, "No," it is rape.

Many men's definition of rape does not apply to their own behavior or that of their male friends. Many men, as well as many women, honestly believe that men cannot control themselves when they are sexually aroused. They believe the girl or woman is responsible both for arousing and for controlling the man. This is absolute rubbish. At any age, a man is perfectly able to control his sexual drive at any point, from first arousal to climax. However, the attitude that the man is not responsible for his actions with women is not a new idea. Many men, young and old, still have the fantasy that once aroused, they have a right to have sex with a woman, regardless of her wants, desires, or needs.

In a recent seminar at a prominent university fraternity in Georgia, I was amazed at the attitude of the men I was addressing. When asked, "How many's 'No's' does it take before you finally stop your sexual pursuit?" the answer was, "Twenty or thirty." In fact, the president of the fraternity actually said, "If we give women the right to say 'No,' it gives them too much power." But, this kind of attitude is not exclusive to young college males. I was shocked when I gave a similar talk at a local church's non-denominational singles group. The participants were middle-aged, successful adults, including doctors, lawyers, and business executives. One actually stood up and said: "If a woman gets in my Mercedes without wearing a bra, she's asking for it!" Another man agreed, saying that any woman who goes up to a man's apartment, or allows a man into her apartment, is saying she wants to have sex. Such attitudes have been created by and taught by fathers, grandfathers, and yes, even mothers. Some women today still believe that it's a woman's job to control the man's behavior, and that women just have to tolerate the assaults.

Rape is about power. Men rape to get power over women. These men may feel powerless in their lives and so look for a way to increase their sense of self-worth by controlling and manipulating another "weaker" human being. Of course, this is a flawed idea, and rape doesn't give the rapist any lasting sense of power or self-worth, so he may continue to commit the crime until it becomes increasingly violent.

Reality Check: All rapists are serial rapists—they rape until they are stopped, averaging four to five rapes. They rarely get help themselves, i.e., they don't stop until they're stopped.

Let's be clear about this point of control. A woman is not responsible for keeping a man in control of his own sexual responses. Each man is responsible for his own actions and no matter what a woman does, he has no right to any sexual contact with her against her will or without her knowledge. Rape is not just "he said/she said." Rape is not just a misunderstanding or the result of a lack of communication. Rape is an act of choice to commit a crime, to forcibly obtain power over another individual through the means of sexual assault.

Reality Check: Rape is not just a misunderstanding. Rape is a criminal act of choosing to overpower a woman and impose sexual intercourse on her without her consent or without her knowledge.

A false sense of security

The term "date/acquaintance rape" is used today to mean any situation in which the assailant merely is known to the victim. It should be understood that just because a woman is not dating the perpetrator doesn't mean he can't be a date/acquaintance rapist. Any man who has access to a woman can commit rape, including her doctor, lawyer, pastor, teacher, delivery man, salesman, brother, father, or friend.

Reality Check: You are five times more likely to be raped by someone you know than by a stranger.

All women, no matter their ages, should remember that being desperate for companionship or willing to settle for any relationship in order not to be alone could lead to dangerous situations. Younger women put themselves at risk because they may not realize the potential for danger. More mature women may derive a false sense of security from their past dating experience and feel they are "older and wiser."

Date/acquaintance rape has touched nearly every college/university campus. Some educators, school officials, security staffs, and counselors are at a loss as to how to talk about stopping date rape without appearing to say that the university environment is unsafe. The reality is that a university is no more dangerous than any other high-density environment. However, many students approach this community environment with little or no awareness of the possible dangers.

First-year students are caught up with being on their own away from home. Tragically, the thrill of that freedom supersedes any thought that crime, specifically sexual assault, can happen to them. Most of the time, the excitement of having her own place as well as the determination to "make it" without parental controls can silence the real dangers of being a single woman on her own. The euphoria of living away from home on a college campus can create a false sense of security. For this reason, young women often get into situations, usually with alcohol and/or drugs, in which they are easy prey for more experienced men. It is common for students to take unnecessary risks while at school, because they feel invulnerable and protected in the college environment. In addition, young women may want to have a good time and party with alcohol just like the guys. This can be a dangerous mistake.

Rape is not just a misunderstanding . . . [it] is an act of choice to commit a crime.

Mature women believe they can let their guard down because they have dated before. The dynamics of starting a new relationship can be very difficult, especially if the woman is dating again for the first time in many years. Beyond the ready-made social environment of a university campus, it can be more difficult to meet eligible men to date. Loneliness or insecurity may cause a woman to go out with men she might not ordinarily consider a good match, or she might meet men through personal ads or at singles bars where she really won't know anything about them before the dating begins. To some degree, a mature woman can use this to her advantage, as she is less likely to think she knows the man well after only a few encounters than a college student who may be fooled by the apparent safety of her campus environment. Although she's had more dating experience, a more mature woman may have forgotten the realities of being with a "stranger." Fears, insecurities, and family may complicate even the simplest of friendships. If she's going out with someone after a long marriage of twenty or thirty years, she may find out quickly that times have changed. She will need to think about her own physical safety and take the same precautions that a younger woman should take.

A false sense of intimacy, misleading appearances

Thinking she knows a man after only one or two encounters, or after seeing him only in public, can place a woman in jeopardy. Familiarity breeds a dropping of one's guard. We are taught as youngsters to fear strangers, but not friends and acquaintances. Yet, we are in far greater danger from those we know (or think we know) than from a stranger. It is especially inconceivable to a young, naive woman that she could be assaulted by the very guy who shares her classes with her. Even a more mature woman, if she wants a relationship badly, will ignore her instincts and perhaps forgo cautionary behaviors in order to give herself a green light for the relationship. Remember, you never really can know an individual in one or two encounters. It is essential for women to observe a person in a variety of social situations over a period of time before allowing herself to be in a vulnerable situation with him.

Appearances can be deceptive and are, unfortunately, not a foolproof indicator of what may be going on below the surface. The majority of rapists are middle-class white men. Neat clothing and grooming may be reassuring, but it is more to the point to inquire into a man's attitudes towards women and to carefully observe how he treats you.

The rapist desires power more than sex. We tend to think that men who are desirable and attractive can't be rapists. Not true. These kind of men can be just as mixed up about sexual coercion as less desirable men. The average rapist is not a twisted, ugly monster who lurks in the bushes. The average rapist looks like, and maybe is, the guy next door.

Drinking, taking drugs, and becoming isolated

The vast majority of date and acquaintance rapes involve abuse of alcohol and/or drugs. . . . However, it is a fact that alcohol affects women differently than men. This disparity is due mainly to three factors: body size, body composition, and levels of alcohol dehydrogenase enzyme. On average, women are smaller than men and carry more body fat, which contains little water to dilute alcohol in the bloodstream. In addition, women have less of the metabolizing enzyme alcohol dehydrogenase. Together, these differences between male and female physiology result in a higher concentration of alcohol in a woman's body than in a man's, for the same amount of alcohol ingested. A woman, generally speaking, will become more intoxicated on less alcohol than a man will.

Women [should] observe a person in a variety of social situations . . . before allowing herself [sic] to be in a vulnerable situation with him.

Criminals generally don't commit their crimes in view of the public. Likewise, a rapist will want to isolate his victim before he commits the crime. If a man attempts to sexually assault his date in a fairly public place, she stands a better chance of attracting attention and getting help than if she is alone with him. In order to prevent herself from becoming isolated, a woman must stay alert and plan ahead for how she would respond if the guy she is with shows signs of becoming dangerous. She must mentally prepare for that possibility.

Ignoring warning signals

What are the warning signals that a man sends when he intends to take advantage of a woman? There is more to this than just the "nagging feeling" that you have in the pit of your stomach that something is wrong. In his book, *The Gift of Fear*, Gavin de Becker, the world's foremost violence prevention specialist, outlines the behaviors criminals use on women. You should be careful if the man you are with does any of the following:

- Behaves as if the two of you are more intimate than you really are, or uses a lot of "we" phrases and appears to be working too hard to make you trust him.
- Appears to be trying to charm you, i.e., disorient you or allure you.

"Niceness is a decision, a strategy of social intercourse. It is not a character trait. It has been said that men are nice when they pursue, women are nice when they reject," says de Becker. Behaving in a way that is unusual or excessively ingratiating can be a sign that a man is attempting to manipulate or control you.

- Gives too many details about himself. If he is giving you information that you are not asking for, and that most people would not volunteer, he may be lying to you.
- Makes slight criticisms and offers you the opportunity to prove him wrong. For example, if a man says: "You're so beautiful that you are probably stuck up and wouldn't go out with someone like me," he may be hoping you'll say to yourself, "I'm not a snob, and I'll prove him wrong by going out with him." This is manipulation, as the man may be trying to get you to think going out with him is your idea, and that you have something to prove to him.
- Spends lavishly on you and appears to be expecting something in return. If the man is attempting to make you feel that you owe him something, you may be in for trouble.
- Makes unsolicited promises, such as, "I'll just have one drink, and then I'll go." An unsolicited promise can be a way to buy time or to give the man an opportunity to get control over you or the situation. If you have made it clear that you want your date to leave, and he says he'll leave "just as soon as I have another drink," or, "after I use the bathroom," or, "after I make a phone call," etc., you will have to be firm and communicate clearly and strongly your desire to leave or for him to leave.
- Attempts to control you. If your date is not allowing you to participate in decisions about the date, if he insists on ordering for you in a restaurant, on "taking care of everything," or suggests that you don't trust him, these may be warning signals.
- Says derogatory things about women. Expressing an attitude that women are inferior to men, that women should obey men, or that women are responsible for a man's sexual response can all be signs of trouble.
- Doesn't accept "No" for an answer. If he offers you a drink, or suggests that you go somewhere with him, and continues to press you even after you say, "No" you will have to be very firm and communicate very clearly. If he won't accept "No," for an answer on something small, he may not in regard to sex, either.

Ignoring her inner guidance

We live in a male-dominated culture that often debunks intuition and inner guidance. Women who trust their inner guidance may be ridiculed by men for not being logical and realistic. The truth is that your inner guidance or intuition is the most trustworthy and dependable barometer. The above manipulations and tactics that most criminals use also can be used by perfectly harmless men. So the problem is, how does a woman know when one or more of these techniques is being used by a man with dangerous intentions? The answer lies in her intuition. When it comes to danger, intuition is always right in at least two important ways: (1) It is responding to something real. (2) It has your best interests at heart.

The following levels of intuition will give you an idea of how intuition works. According to de Becker, your intuition builds from curiosity to hunches, to gut feelings, to doubt, to hesitation, to suspicion, to apprehension, and finally to fear. Fear is the most important and critical. If you feel fear in a situation, honor it.

If he won't accept "No," for an answer on something small, he may not in regard to sex, either.

The question then arises, "What makes a woman *in*vulnerable?" It is not so much a question of invulnerability, since all of us are vulnerable to crime. It is rather a question of what makes a woman stronger and less likely to become a victim? The answer is knowledge, combined with a determination to act in her own best interest, regardless of what others think or do.

2

Date Rape Is a Serious Crime

Sherry F. Colb

Sherry F. Colb is a professor of law at Rutgers Law School in New Jersey. She is a frequent contributor to Writ, *an online newsletter focused on legal issues, from which the following viewpoint was selected.*

The majority of rapes fall into the category of date/acquaintance rape, in which the victim knows her attacker. Many people, however, remain unconvinced that date/acquaintance rape is a serious offense. Studies on the effects of date rape tell a different story—rape victims who know their attackers experience longer periods of psychological trauma than victims raped by strangers. The American justice system should treat date/acquaintance rape as a crime with real consequences for offenders.

In my first-year criminal law class at Rutgers, we are now covering the unit on rape. Because the subject implicates the roles of gender and sexuality in a free society, it poses distinct challenges in the classroom.

Law professor Susan Estrich—the author of the book *Real Rape*—observed in 1986 that "[t]o examine rape within the criminal law tradition is to expose fully the sexism of the law." Though she wrote this fifteen years ago, attitudes have not evolved as much as one might have hoped. In particular, mainstream perceptions of acquaintance rape, or "date rape," remain extremely troubling.

Date rape portrayed as a trivial offense

Last Friday morning [early November 2001], for example, I picked up the "Weekend" section of the *New York Times*. I thought it would be pleasant to read about something other than war and terror. I chose a review of a movie called *Tape*, directed by Richard Linklater. The review was positive, and the movie sounded intriguing. As a professor teaching rape law and as a woman, however, I found the article quite disturbing.

Tape, according to the review, is about two former high school classmates and the girl they both used to love. During the course of a tension-filled verbal power struggle between the men, it emerges that one of them raped the girl they had both dated.

Though the reviewer enjoyed the film, he nonetheless identifies what he sees as a flaw in the story: "As incisive as *Tape* is," he says, "it is ultimately limited by the moral weight of the deed under consideration and the sexual politics swirling around the subject. This wasn't a murder, after all, but sex forced on a woman who admits she was in love with the man who took advantage of her. . . . To put it bluntly, it is very small potatoes."

Reading this movie review reminded me that many in the mainstream remain unconvinced that the rape of an acquaintance—what some call "date rape"—is a serious offense. Such a perspective presents a problem, because most rapes fall into this category.

Rape victims who previously knew their attackers take longer to begin to recover from the psychological trauma of the crime.

Indeed, according to the U.S. Department of Justice, three out of four victims of sexual assault had a prior relationship with their respective attackers. If having had a relationship vitiates the severity of the offense, then the overwhelming majority of rape crimes are "small potatoes."

The movie reviewer in question was a man, but men are not the only people who take the view he expresses. Generation-X author Katie Rolphe became famous for writing that much of what prudish feminists call "rape" is not actually rape at all but just bad sex that women regret after the fact. Other writers like Camille Paglia have suggested that resisting a man's sexual advances does not convert his subsequent behavior into rape; it is all just part of the game.

Date rape perceived as a "victimless" crime

Rape is not unique among crimes in triggering controversy as to whether (in certain circumstances) it should qualify as a serious crime. Many have criticized laws that ban drug possession and prostitution, for example, and there are even organizations devoted to the repeal of these laws.

The difference, though, is that proponents of legalizing drug possession and prostitution can plausibly claim that these are "victimless" crimes, and that prosecuting them does more harm than good. Rape, by contrast, is never victimless. Those who perceive the crime as "small potatoes" thus demonstrate a profound failure of empathy.

The kind of rape that most people take seriously involves a man who attacks a woman he neither knows, nor has reason to believe has any interest in him. When it comes to date rape, however, people are skeptical of victims' allegations and dubious about the weight of the offense, even if it did occur.

The reason for such skepticism and doubt is the possibility that the victim might have liked her assailant. If she did, some believe, then having him force himself on her could not have been that bad.

As the movie reviewer described it, the rapist under such circumstances would have only "taken advantage" of his victim—the sort of manners offense that an eager salesperson might commit against a customer who really would have preferred not to buy the most expensive suit on the rack.

The reality of the crime of date rape

This view of rape, however, bears no relation to the reality of the crime for its victims. Indeed, the very types of attacks that people minimize may have the most devastating impact.

Studies have shown that rape victims who previously knew their attackers take longer to begin to recover from the psychological trauma of the crime than those who were raped by strangers.

Now that we live in an age of terrorism, this phenomenon should not surprise anyone. The closer we are to a familiar environment when tragedy strikes, the less safe we feel in what was previously "home." What is true for the physical spaces of our lives is equally true for our relationships.

This is one reason why many consider incest against children a worse offense than child molestation by a stranger. The law normally recognizes that the people in whom we place our trust bear an added responsibility not to betray it.

Rape is arguably worse than murder, because the attacker has . . . both killed his victim and made a survivor out of her.

When someone we love, someone in whom we trust, hurts us, it is uniquely damaging because it shakes the foundations of our sense of security. When we would normally retreat to the familiar for comfort, it is the familiar that frightens us most.

We also come to doubt our ability to distinguish between friend and foe, between safety and danger—because after all, we were the ones who chose the company of our own enemy. (This further aggravates the insidious tendency of women to blame themselves for their own date rapes, on the logic that after all, they should have known better than to date such a man, or to dress provocatively, and so on.)

The movie reviewer was right that rape "after all" is not murder. The Supreme Court indeed held in *Coker v. Georgia* that capital punishment is an excessive penalty for rape, precisely because the rape victim survives. But the fact that rape is not murder does not diminish the gravity of the crime.

Like survivors of any disaster, rape victims continue to suffer long after the physical ordeal has passed. As one of my students said in analyzing *Coker*, rape is arguably worse than murder, because the attacker has, in some sense, both killed his victim and made a survivor out of her.

Teaching rape amidst the controversy

A former colleague of mine once told me that he chooses not to teach rape law at all, because it is the one crime of which he is sure that there will be survivors in the classroom who could become upset by the material.

This is a real concern and one that I do not take lightly. I nonetheless resolve the matter the other way, because I think that cutting the material out of the syllabus communicates to students that this crime—one which alters forever the lives of its victims—does not "count" as much as manslaughter and robbery do.

By covering the law of rape, in all its complexity and controversy, I hope to convey to students that the crime is neither invisible nor insignificant. Rather, it is important and worthy of our attention, both as attorneys and attorneys-to-be and as members of a civilized society that aspires to equality for women.

3

Rape Is Too Broadly Defined

Cathy Young

Cathy Young is a journalist and the author of Ceasefire! Why Women and Men Must Join Forces to Achieve True Equality, *from which this viewpoint is taken. She is cofounder of the Women's Freedom Network, a forum for moderate feminists, and a research associate with the Cato Institute, a libertarian think tank.*

Definitions of what constitutes rape have become overly broad and unclear. Force or threats of bodily harm, factors that defined rape prior to the "date rape" movement, are no longer considered relevant to many anti-rape activists—if explicit consent for sex was not granted by the woman, then a man has committed rape. Calling instances of sexual miscommunication rape trivializes real rape in which a woman's life is truly in jeopardy. Due to pressure from feminist groups, many states have begun to make sexual assault without force or threat a serious crime based solely on the woman's "no." The downside of this newly expanded definition of rape is that defendants in rape cases can now be convicted on flimsy evidence.

> Politically, I call it rape whenever a woman has sex and feels violated.
> —Catharine MacKinnon, *Feminism: Unmodified*

The debate about rape and the law is complicated by the fact that there doesn't seem to be much agreement anymore on what rape is. We can all agree (I hope) that a person always has the right to say no, no matter how far things have gone, and no one has the right to force sex on another. But what does that mean? Take this scenario from a college pamphlet:

> A couple have been going out for a while and have had sex before. After a dinner date, they return to his place where he begins to take off her clothes. She pushes him back, saying "no" . . . he pulls her firmly against him, says "yes" and continues to undress her. They have intercourse.

Calling it rape: "no means no" and beyond

Is this rape? I have no idea. Does she try to get out of his embrace? Does he restrain her? Does she push him away again and tell him, "I said, no"? Or does she eagerly await his caresses?

What if a woman is in bed with her lover and says that she just wants to talk, but her lover keeps touching and caressing her, and she finally gives in and fakes an orgasm? Such a story ran in 1992 in the Massachusetts Institute of Technology paper, the *Thistle*, under the title, "When She Says No, It's *Always* Rape." (The "rapist," by the way, was another woman.) When I showed the article to Virginia MacKay-Smith, an assistant dean at Harvard and a leader of the university's Date Rape Task Force, she was positive that if a student came to her with such a complaint, she would "feel no hesitation to report it to the police" or bring administrative charges.

What if the woman says no and the man threatens to dump her or "makes fun of her for being a prude"? According to a 1997 article in a popular magazine for teenage girls, he's a date rapist using "psychological intimidation."

[Date rape] activists routinely blur the lines between actual violence and "emotional coercion."

And what about drunken sex? Clearly, if a man takes advantage of a woman who has passed out, that's rape. But there are also situations like the one described in a letter to Ann Landers by a woman who met a man in a bar and ended up in bed with him after two drinks, only to feel disgusted with herself the next morning: "I phoned my girlfriend and told her what happened. She said, 'You were raped.' I told her I didn't see it that way." Amazingly, Ann replies: "Yes, your friend is right." (Are people commonly absolved of responsibility for their actions because they've had a couple of drinks?)

In a 1991 essay rebuking "apologists for date rape," writer Susan Jacoby recalled an episode from her youth. Involved in a troubled relationship, depressed and confused, she invited an ex-boyfriend over for a sexual interlude—and changed her mind on the way to the bedroom. That he didn't force himself on her but simply left in a huff, she wrote, was no more than should be expected of a civilized human being. Readily conceding that some women enjoy being coy and some men enjoy coaxing a woman further than she meant to go, Jacoby stressed that these games have nothing to do with rape: one can easily tell the difference "between a half-hearted 'no, we shouldn't' and tears or screams; between a woman who is physically free to leave a room and one who is being physically restrained."

Jacoby is right, but she wrongly credits the anti–date rape activists with the same common sense. To them, "no means no" makes no allowances for tone of voice. MacKay-Smith, the Harvard dean, told me that a distinction between a half-hearted "no" and tears and screams "opens the door to a lot of interpretation and a lot of harm." Kathryn Geller Myers of the Pennsylvania Coalition Against Rape said that "after the first 'no,' there should be no progression of seduction or whatever";

anything that follows is rape. Does this mean that once you say no, your partner has no right to try to change your mind? "That's exactly what I'm saying," replied Myers.

Blurring the lines

Imagine what would happen if we were to apply these principles to other areas of life. If a friend nagged you into lending him your car, we would call it acquaintance carjacking. If someone talked you into going on an unwanted trip by making you feel guilty about refusing, that would be kidnapping. If a relative from out of town wanted to stay at your place and did not take repeated hints that this wasn't such a good time, that would be no different from thugs forcing their way in at gunpoint.

Robin Warshaw, whose 1988 book *I Never Called It Rape* is a bible of date rape activism, insists in the foreword to the 1994 edition that date rape is nothing less than forced sex, involving physical coercion, threats, or incapacitation (even if the victim doesn't consider it rape). Dismissing concerns about overbroad definitions of rape as "backlash" and "rape-denial," Warshaw admits that she has seen "occasional materials" using such definitions. She forgets to mention that among those materials is a text to which she contributed, and which she lists among the resources at the end of her book. The 1991 volume *Acquaintance Rape: The Hidden Crime* includes, under the heading "Types of Acquaintance Rape," an essay on "Nonviolent Sexual Coercion," defined as "verbal arguments not including verbal threats of force" such as "everyone's doing it."

Nor does Warshaw acknowledge that some widely publicized studies of date rape use the term loosely. A campus survey by Stanford University's Rape Education Project generated such headlines as, "Date Rape Common, Stanford Study Says; 33% of Women, 12% of Men Tell of Forced Sex." These findings were understandably characterized as "shocking." Yet aside from the fact that a mere 10 percent of the "victims" believed they were raped, 75 percent of this "forced sex" involved "continual arguments and pressure," and another 10 percent involved alcohol.

One can't keep saying that "rape is a life-threatening situation" and using the word for situations in which no threat to life exists.

I wonder if Warshaw, whose own experience of acquaintance rape was a brutal assault by a knife-wielding ex-lover, is troubled when someone like Katie Koestner emerges as a spokeswoman for the anti–date rape movement. A graduate of the College of William and Mary who now lectures on sexual violence, Koestner became a media darling when she went public as a victim of date rape. Yet she acknowledges that the young man she accused did nothing more than keep pressing for sex despite her repeated refusals, and even that she didn't say "no" immediately prior to intercourse.

The activists routinely blur the lines between actual violence and "emotional coercion." "No one has the right to verbally pressure or physically force you to have sex," states a leaflet of the Bergen County Rape Crisis Center in New Jersey. Of the respondents to a survey my research assistant sent to rape crisis centers, two-thirds said it was rape if a man got a woman into bed by using emotional pressure but no force or threats of bodily harm. Some elaborated: "Yes, such as threatening to leave her." Even if the woman never said "no" because she didn't want to hurt his feelings, many would treat her as a rape victim. One of the few people in the field to have publicly criticized these views—Gillian Greensite, director of the rape prevention program at the University of California at Santa Cruz—says that she has encountered "real hostility and narrow-mindedness" from her colleagues.

For many activists, the strictest interpretation of "no means no" is not enough: nothing less than an explicit "yes" will do. The notorious Antioch College sexual offense code, which mandates verbal consent every step of the way, from undoing a button to penetration, may be unique, but many colleges and universities have instituted less extreme versions of such policies. In 1994, a senior at Pomona College in California was nearly prevented from graduating because of a rape complaint brought with a two-year delay. The woman admitted that she willingly went to his room after a party, let him undress her, and never said no—but claimed that she never gave her consent, defined by the school as "clear, explicit agreement to engage in a specific activity."

Negotiating sex

Katha Pollitt's vitriolic review of *The Morning After*, Katie Roiphe's critique of "rape-crisis feminism," was titled "Not Just Bad Sex." But some feminist theorists are candid about their view that the date rape crusade *is* about bad sex. Philosopher Lois Pineau, who believes that good sex is "communicative sex," would require the accused man to prove that he took steps not only to ensure the woman's explicit consent but to find out "what she liked," since "it is not reasonable for women to consent" otherwise. (Columnist Ellen Goodman thinks it's a brilliantly provocative idea.) Others suggest that requiring women to give verbal consent to sex is a good way to subvert the convention of female passivity, though they still assume that it's the man who will do the asking, while the woman is relieved even from the responsibility of fending off unwanted advances.

Of course, there is always communication in sex; it just doesn't have to involve words. A physical overture is a nonverbal request for permission to proceed; the response is a nonverbal "yes" or "no." Most people, women or men, have a visceral aversion to communicating sexual intent directly; even code-abiding Antioch students reportedly resort to the wry euphemism, "Want to activate the policy?" Partly it's because we want to camouflage the vulnerability that comes from expressing sexual need; partly because, as women's magazines often point out when warning about the baneful effects of self-consciousness about one's body, good sex is about letting go. This does not mean that, as Katha Pollitt caricatures the position of verbal consent critics, talk in intimate encounters kills eroticism; but lucid, clear-headed negotiations certainly do.

"No means no" absolutism is just as far removed from real life. In a 1988 study by feminist researcher Charlene Muehlenhard, 60 percent of sexually active college women admitted that they had on occasion said "no" while fully intending to have sex; nearly all had said "no" when they weren't sure. (A woman could also say no and mean it, and then change her mind.) Psychologists Lucia O'Sullivan and Elizabeth Allgeier have found that not only young women but young men use "token resistance" in sexual situations—to avoid being seen as interested just in sex, to slow things down out of concern for the relationship, to add spice and challenge to the mating dance. Three-quarters of men and women alike regarded these interactions as enjoyable.

In response to the outcry from feminists, Pennsylvania politicians [passed] . . . a bill making sexual assault without force or threat . . . a second-degree felony.

Both Muehlenhard and some feminist commentators who acknowledge her inconvenient findings insist that even if many women say "no" when they don't really mean it, men should still be punished for ignoring a woman's "no" when she does mean it. (This argument speaks volumes about their belief that only men should be held responsible for sexual miscommunication.) But does the belief that "no" doesn't always mean no put women in danger of rape, as these scholars suggest? These fears are not supported by a poll in which 60 percent of young men said they would *not* stop immediately "in the heat of passion" if the woman said "no"; the vast majority said they would stop if she sounded upset or said "no" more than once, and virtually all the rest said they would stop if she resisted physically.

Trivializing real rape

Feminists are free to advocate "communicative" sex with no ambiguity and no loss of control. They certainly have every right to say that it's wrong to pressure a reluctant partner into unwanted sex; most people would agree. The problem is that the debate about proper sexual norms has been framed as a debate about rape. As critics have pointed out, this trivializes real rape: one can't keep saying that "rape is a life-threatening situation" and using the word for situations in which no threat to life exists. (One paradox most feminists sidestep is that when "nonviolent sexual coercion" is redefined as rape, many men qualify as victims of rape by women.)

But "calling it rape," to borrow the title of a play widely performed on college campuses in the 1990s, has its advantages for the advocates: it chills the debate about sexual norms. When a sexual assault counselor warns that "the blind give-and-take of sexual negotiations" can lead to "game playing, deception, and confusion," one can say, "That's life." But when he asks, "Isn't rape prevention important enough for us to . . . modify our behavior?" one can't easily say "no."

The rape label also places what many feminists consider nonconsensual sex within the scope of the law (or sanctions by college panels). The advocates' power rests on intimidation, not persuasion. In a list of "Ten Reasons to Obtain Verbal Consent to Sex," Bernice Sandler, head of the

National Association of Women in Education, quickly goes from the dubious assertion that "many partners find it sexy to be asked, as sex pro-
gresses, if it's okay" to "you won't go to jail or be expelled."

Force and consent: the legal debate

The criminal law ought to say clearly that women who actually say no must be respected as meaning it; that nonconsent means saying no; that men who proceed nonetheless . . . have acted unreasonably and unlawfully.
                              —Susan Estrich, *Yale Law Journal*

The strict construction of "no means no" has made significant inroads into
the justice system in the last two decades. Curiously, the *Yale Law Journal*
article titled "Rape" by then–Harvard Law School professor Susan Estrich,
and her subsequent book, *Real Rape*, which played a seminal role in the development of legal thinking on the issue, never addressed situations in
which the man proceeds with nonforcible advances after the woman says
"no." Estrich's examples were of women who were clearly in fear. In *State
v. Rusk*, a Maryland case from the late 1970s, the woman gave the man a
ride home from a bar and reluctantly followed him into the house after he
took her car keys. She testified that she tearfully begged him to let her go,
but he "kept saying 'no.'" Finally, she asked, "If I do what you want, will
you let me go without killing me?" and gave in after he said yes.

The man's conviction was upheld, but three of the seven appellate
judges dissented because the woman did such a poor job of defending her
virtue. The victim's submission, they wrote, had to "stem from fear generated by something of substance." Yet surely what is wrong here is not the
argument itself but the view that being in a strange neighborhood at night,
with a man who won't let you leave, is not a substantial cause for fear.

In 1986, when Estrich's essay appeared, the California Supreme Court
ruled, in *People v. Barnes*, another case in which the woman gave in without a fight. The defendant's methods of persuasion after she rebuffed him
included grabbing her by the collar, bragging that he could "pick her up
with one hand and throw her out," and warning her not to upset him.
The court affirmed that even without resistance, sexual intercourse "by
means of force or fear of immediate and unlawful bodily injury" was rape.
This position wasn't very different from the *Rusk* dissent; it simply
showed a better understanding of reasonable fear.

It's interesting to compare this to a controversial Pennsylvania case a
few years later. Robert Berkowitz, a junior at East Stroudsburg University,
was accused of raping a nineteen-year-old sophomore. The young
woman, who was dating another student but had previously engaged
Berkowitz in rather explicit sexual banter, had come to his dorm room
looking for his roommate, who was out. They sat on the floor and talked
about her man troubles; then Berkowitz leaned over and started kissing
her and fondling her breasts, despite her protestations that she had to go
and meet her boyfriend. According to the young woman, she said "no"
in a "scolding" tone but never tried to push him away or get up (by her
own account, she was not pinned down). Berkowitz admitted that he
heard her whisper "no" but claimed that she returned his kisses, moan-

ing "amorously." She made no attempt to leave when he went to lock the door, which, as she knew, could still be opened from the inside with a simple turn of the knob.

By her account, Berkowitz then "put [her] down on the bed" and removed her pants while she was "kind of laying there"; after he entered her, she softly moaned "no." Again, he confirmed the "no" but also claimed that the young woman moaned "passionately" and helped him undress her; after they started having sex, he noticed a "blank look on her face" and asked what was wrong. (They both agreed that he withdrew and ejaculated in about thirty seconds.) The girl told her boyfriend what happened, and he called the police.

The notion of the special credibility of rape complainants is gaining a foothold in the criminal justice system.

Berkowitz was found guilty. However, an appellate court reversed his conviction, concluding that there was no evidence of "forcible compulsion." When the Pennsylvania State Supreme Court upheld this ruling in 1994, women's groups were up in arms. The media hewed the party line, often condensing the facts in a way that made them seem less ambiguous. Activists blasted the court for telling victims that they had to "physically resist and risk serious bodily injury." Yet the ruling specifically noted that the victim "need not resist" when there is force or threats to induce submission.

"I did . . . what everyone taught us to do in college," Berkowitz's "victim" told a local paper. "If we were being raped, say 'no' and don't fight, because you could wind up dead." Although studies suggest that fighting back may improve women's chances of avoiding rape without raising the risk of injury, a rape victim (like a robbery victim) certainly should not be *required* by law to resist a violent assault. But was there a violent assault in *Berkowitz*—or was the young woman the victim of a date rape education that never explained the difference between rape and persistent, nonviolent sexual advances? She herself had admitted that she was not threatened. There was, as the court stressed, no evidence that she "could not have walked out . . . without any risk of harm or danger to herself." Susan Estrich herself found the case troubling: "Is a man guilty of rape if a woman says no but just doesn't bother to leave?"

Yet in response to the outcry from feminists, Pennsylvania politicians were quick to pass a bill making sexual assault without force or threat, based solely on a "no," a second-degree felony punishable by up to ten years in prison. In other states, too, the law has been inching closer to the hard-line interpretation of "no means no."

In 1994, three weeks after the *Berkowitz* ruling, the Colorado Court of Appeals explicitly rejected the reasoning of the Pennsylvania court and affirmed a conviction in such a case by a two-to-one vote. The woman had claimed that the defendant not only ignored her "no" but overpowered her in a violent struggle. The jury rejected this story, which was contradicted by physical evidence, and acquitted Gregory Schmidt of first-degree sexual assault, which requires the use or threat of force, but they convicted him of second-degree sexual assault: penetration by any other means "reasonably calculated to cause submission against the victim's will." This verdict, the court of appeals said, was supported by Schmidt's own story that after "messing around," the woman said no to sex (mainly for fear of being found out by his wife) and that he still pulled off her panties and had sex with her, assuming that everything was fine since she didn't protest again. What did he do to cause her unwilling submission? The court resolved this question simply: once permission is denied, *anything* the defendant does to obtain sex fits the bill.

Most rape statutes still require force or threat, but that hardly settles the issue. In a 1992 ruling, the New Jersey State Supreme Court managed to turn a law defining sexual assault as penetration by "physical force or coercion" into an Antioch-style explicit consent requirement.

Fifteen-year-old C.G. claimed that she woke up at night to find herself being assaulted by M.T.S., a seventeen-year-old boy lodging at her mother's house. According to M.T.S., she had invited him to bed and willingly engaged in kissing and fondling, but became very upset when he "stuck it in." By both accounts, he stopped and left immediately after she slapped his face and verbally rebuked him. C.G.'s mother took her to the police the next day, after the girl said that M.T.S. had raped her and she wanted him out of the house. At the trial, the judge concluded that the girl's story of sleeping soundly while being stripped of her shorts and underpants was implausible, and that the boy probably told the truth—but that he was guilty anyway, since she had consented to "heavy petting," not to sex. (As a juvenile, M.T.S. was sentenced to probation and a small fine.)

The conviction was set aside on appeal, on the grounds that the element of force was missing—and then reinstated by the New Jersey State Supreme Court, which held unanimously that without "affirmative and freely-given permission," penetration itself constituted force. The court did vaguely suggest that permission could be granted through "physical actions." But it repeatedly stressed that the victim "need not have said or done anything" to deny consent, and no questions can be asked about why she didn't protest.

Proof and credibility

Broadly or narrowly defined, rape can still be difficult to prove or disprove. In the past, the accuser's testimony had to be corroborated by other evidence—a rule that, feminists not unreasonably argued, was discriminatory, since no corroboration was required for robbery or assault. Yet only a minority of jurisdictions ever strictly enforced this requirement—often a "prompt outcry" was considered sufficient to meet it—and by 1980, it was virtually extinct.

Just because corroboration is not legally necessary does not mean that it's unimportant; without it, a conviction is far less likely for any crime. Interestingly, in her 1986 article, Estrich rejected the claim that rape was treated differently from other serious crimes: "The downgrading of cases involving prior relationships, less force, and no corroboration is characteristic of the criminal justice system." But in rape cases, Estrich wrote, "corroboration may be uniquely absent": there are usually no eyewitnesses, no material evidence—such as a weapon in a felony assault or the loot in a robbery—and no injury if the victim is too frightened to resist. Therefore, she concluded, giving "equal weight" to corroboration for rape, robbery, and assault was not "neutral" but actually unfair to rape victims.

But then it follows that, to be "fair," *we should convict defendants in rape cases on less evidence and give the complaint's word more weight than in other crimes.* And that makes all those old misogynistic warnings about how difficult it is for an innocent man to defend himself against a charge of rape seem uncomfortably close to the truth.

Yet the notion of the special credibility of rape complainants is gaining a foothold in the criminal justice system. Sometimes it is even codified in law.

In California since the 1900s, juries were told that a rape defendant could be convicted on the accuser's word alone, balancing the warning to treat her testimony with caution. Although the cautionary instruction was eliminated in 1975, the other one survived. In 1992, attorneys appealing a conviction in a her-word-against-his case argued that this gave the prosecution an unfair edge: since jurors were also admonished to review carefully any claim based on the word of a single witness, to stress that the complainant's testimony was sufficient could suggest that she was entitled to more credit than other witnesses, including the defendant. The California Supreme Court disagreed, opining that the instruction was still needed to counteract prejudice against rape victims. By then, rape cases tried in California had a 92 percent conviction rate, just behind homicide.

For some modern juries, it seems to take a great deal to override the credibility of a woman who says she was raped. In 1996, Michael Ivers, a junior at Michigan State University, was tried on charges of sexually assaulting a first-year student he had met at an off-campus party. Ivers testified that they went back to his apartment and had consensual sex; the young woman claimed that she had an alcoholic blackout and remembered nothing from the moment they left the party together to the moment she found herself in bed with him. One might say her word against his left plenty of reasonable doubt: an intoxicated person can forget a block of time without losing consciousness. But in this case, it was her word against his and two others'. Ivers's roommates testified that they came into the room and turned on the lights three different times while the young woman was there, and that she was fully conscious—once even asking that the lights be turned off—and did not ask for help. Nonetheless, Ivers was convicted.

4

A Broader Definition
of Rape Is Necessary

Molly Dragiewicz

Molly Dragiewicz is a professor of women's studies at George Mason University in Virginia.

The term "acquaintance rape" enables women to describe non-consensual sexual encounters that do not fit the stereotypical concept of rape as a violent physical assault committed by a stranger. Following a 1987 study that identified acquaintance rape as a significant problem, mainstream periodicals initially covered acquaintance rape with calls for action. Beginning in the early 1990s, the media and cultural conservatives embarked on a backlash against this broader definition of rape. Backlash proponents contend that if a woman did not physically resist a sexual encounter, then it should be considered consensual sex and not a "real rape." Limiting the use of the word "rape" to violent assaults sends the message that nonconsensual sex—sex that is not wanted on the man's terms—is acceptable, when in fact it is a far more common and equally deplorable form of rape.

Since the 1980s, the terms "acquaintance rape" and "date rape" have come into use to describe sexual assaults that differ from stereotypical Rape concepts. The existence of these terms reveals the substance of dominant ideas about rape. If rape were popularly defined as nonconsensual sex, there would be no need to distinguish between "kinds" (often interpreted as "degrees") of rape, according to the relationship between the rapist and the victim, or the degree of physical force involved. If acquaintance rape were not part of the cultural vocabulary, however, women would currently have no term available to them to describe any rape that differs from dominant connotations of Rape (usually a violent rape committed by a stranger). As a result, many women are forced to use terms that perpetuate the distinction between kinds of rape in order to identify the crime enacted against them as rape at all.

Molly Dragiewicz, "Women's Voices, Women's Words: Reading Acquaintance Rape Discourse," *Feminist Interpretations of Mary Daly*, edited by Sarah Lucia Hoagland and Marilyn Frye. University Park: Pennsylvania State University Press, 2000. Copyright © 2000 by Pennsylvania State University Press. Reproduced by permission.

Consent-based ideas of rape

I am inclined to endorse the use of any term that allows women to name rape as rape, even as I recognize the danger of perpetuating distinctions between "kinds" of rape. That danger stems from the belief that different "kinds" of rape are different in degree as well as in circumstances. The introduction of acquaintance rape into the cultural vocabulary is a move away from definitions of rape that focus on the context of the crime toward definitions that focus on whether the sexual encounter was consensual. The institution of a consent-based idea of rape is a step toward more effectively fighting rape: identifying it as equally deplorable in all of its forms. Thus, the term "acquaintance rape" is presently useful and necessary, even as anti-rape efforts work toward the institution of a consent-based rape concept which would eventually render the term obsolete. . . .

The history of acquaintance rape discourse

The introduction of the term acquaintance rape into the American cultural vocabulary offered the promise of a reformed understanding of rape; one that was more useful to more women in describing rape experiences. News discourse on acquaintance rape is marked by a radical reversal that began in 1990. Before then, scattered coverage of what was variously called "non-stranger rape," "confidence rape," "social rape," "date rape," and "acquaintance rape" appeared in popular magazines. Acquaintance rape coverage proliferated following the publication of "The Scope of Rape: Incidence and Prevalence of Sexual Aggression and Victimization in a National Sample of Higher Education Students" in 1987. Initial media reactions to the study included shock that more rapes were apparently being committed by acquaintances than by strangers, and surprise that such large numbers of female students reported having been victims of assaults matching the legal definition of rape. Mainstream print news media responded to the "Scope of Rape" study with calls for action. Writers of news stories aimed to educate and offered analyses of the causes of acquaintance rape. While conservative publications refused to accept the results of the "Scope of Rape" study all along, many mainstream periodicals concluded that date rape was a problem in need of a solution. It was in mainstream periodicals that the prevalence of rape, and the reality that it is most often perpetrated by acquaintances, was presented to the general public.

The introduction of the term acquaintance rape . . . offered the promise of a reformed understanding of rape.

Since the initial spate of coverage, there has been a reversal of mainstream news opinion on acquaintance rape. This reversal may be viewed as a backlash because it occurred despite the fact that no contradictory research emerged in the period between the initial positive reaction to the "Scope of Rape" study and the ensuing negative coverage. In fact, backlash articles often attack the same study that they cited as definitive a short time earlier. This suggests that the change in coverage of acquaintance rape was not based on new information, but on the political and cultural climate in the United States. Both sides of the debate attribute the backlash to the introduction of the Violence Against Women Act into Congress in 1990. Conservatives such as Neil Gilbert, who call anti-rape efforts "rape hype," have openly stated that their aim was to discredit research on acquaintance rape in order to prevent federal funding of rape-related services. *Newsweek, Time,* and the *New York Times* provide clear illustrations of the reversal of position on acquaintance rape—they all featured articles seeking to educate the public about "date rape" in the mid to late eighties and ran backlash articles in the early nineties.

The initial articles on acquaintance rape validated the research on rape and applauded efforts to decrease rape occurrence. "'Acquaintance Rape' Comes into the Open" appeared in a February 1986 edition of *Newsweek.* The bold type below the headline read, "Colleges work to solve—and stop—a shockingly frequent, often hidden outrage." From there, a brief acquaintance rape scenario was recounted ("Paul ran into his classmate Karen at a dorm party") followed by a definition of acquaintance rape ("forcible sexual assault in which the victim knows her assailant"). Next came arguments about the cause and nature of the crime, and consultations with various experts . . . .

To dismiss women's right to refuse sex as unacceptable [presents] . . . the view that women's consent is largely irrelevant.

In 1991, the *New York Times* led the backlash against efforts to address acquaintance rape, printing Katie Roiphe's Op-Ed piece "Date Rape Hysteria" as a "Voices of a New Generation" feature. The publication of this article provided the backlash with momentum and media attention. Other periodicals (including *Time* and *Newsweek*) soon followed suit. The *New York Times* also printed an expanded version of the Roiphe article "Rape Hype Betrays Feminism" as the cover story for the June 13, 1993, *New York Times Magazine.* Writers of these and other backlash articles use . . . four tactics . . . to subvert the newly emergent discourses on acquaintance rape, which threatened to incite discussion on related, controversial topics. An awareness of the erasure, reversal, false polarization, and divide-and-conquer tactics [based on the theories of renowned feminist Mary Daly] allows readers an opportunity to identify and resist them in discourses on rape and other topics.

Erasure

The first tactic utilized in backlash discourse is erasure. Erasure is manifested in five key ways:

- The dismissal of anti-rape efforts as "sexual correctness"
- The sequestering of the issue of consent
- The naturalization of rape
- The denial of high rape rates
- The subversion of women's authority

First, much backlash discourse feeds on the stigma of "political correctness." A 1993 *Newsweek* cover story on acquaintance rape, titled "Sexual Correctness: Has It Gone Too Far?" appropriates the stigma of political correctness in order to circumvent further discussion on acquaintance rape. The charge of sexual correctness, like that of "political correctness," arises in a reaction against impending changes in the (sexual) status quo, and is intended to derail discussion of the issue at hand.

By erasing women's words, backlash proponents can deny that acquaintance rape is really rape.

The second type of erasure is the erasure of consent, which forces a return to context-based definitions of rape. Focusing on the relationship between the rapist and the victim, on the "character" or past conduct of either, or on the amount of physical violence used during the rape renders the victim's nonconsent a nonissue. Erasure of consent leads to the validation of relationship- or context-based definitions of rape over consent-based definitions. According to context-based definitions of rape, what matters is whether the two people involved knew each other, if they have ever dated, if they have ever had sex before, or if the victim is visibly bruised or injured, all of which are irrelevant to determining whether or not both people consented to a particular sexual encounter.

The erasure of consent is evident in the insistence that we reserve the use of the word rape to describe only stereotypical Rapes, and reject any other definition of rape as "highly original and unacceptably broad," a "paranoid metaphor," an "overused word . . . [a] cliche, drained of specificity and meaning," or a "trendy anti-man, women-as-victim, anti-individual responsibilities P.C. policy." In an attempt to abrogate the significance of consent, backlash discourses describe consent-based definitions of rape as something that "radicalized victims justify flinging around as a political weapon, referring to everything from violent sexual assaults to inappropriate innuendoes," or a "metaphor, its definition swelling to cover any kind of oppression to women." The dismissal of consent-based definitions of rape on the grounds that they are biased in a way that more traditional "objective" definitions of Rape are not is evidence that phallocentric, stereotypical Rape definitions are so prevalent as to be invisible. To dismiss women's right to refuse sex as unacceptable, "paranoid," "anti-man," or "anti-individual responsibilities," is to make a powerful statement about men's absolute authority to define sex and rape, and to present the view that women's consent is largely irrelevant.

Through the erasure of the issue of consent, acquaintance rape itself is erased, and context-based definitions of rape are reaffirmed. Diana Russell discusses the harmful side effects of context-based ideas about rape in her book *The Politics of Rape*. "In cases of rape by friends, it is usually assumed that the victim colludes in her own victimization. It is frequently suggested that the word 'rape' be confined to cases where the woman is raped by a stranger and that another word be invented for cases in which the woman is raped by a friend, acquaintance, lover, or husband. . . . Using the relationship between the rapist and victim as *the* basic distinction between rape experiences can perpetuate . . . the myth of collusion." Russell's observation illustrates the importance of the availability of the term acquaintance rape, given the existing cultural vocabulary. It also explains the dangers of using that term.

The third type of erasure is the naturalization of rape. Timothy Beneke notes that "rape signs" serve to erase rape by including it in our ideas of what is natural or normal. They "stand between us and the reality of rape, obfuscating and numbing our vision and sensitivity. . . . They tell us false stories about rape, men, and women without our consciously hearing the stories." The denial that acquaintance rape is Real Rape is a rape sign, according to Beneke's definition. It naturalizes rapes that do not fit the stranger rape stereotype. The 1991 *Time* article on acquaintance rape exemplifies the naturalization of rape. In response to a statement from Dr. Mary Koss demanding that men be held accountable for committing rape, the *Time* writer argues: "Historically, of course, this has never been the case, and there are some that argue that it shouldn't be—that women too must take responsibility for their behavior, and that the whole realm of intimate encounters defies regulation from on high. Anthropologist Lionel Tiger has little patience for trendy sexual politics that make no reference to biology. Since the dawn of time, he argues, men and women have always gone to bed with different goals." Tiger's assertions naturalize rape by depicting it as a "biological" part of reality. The implication is that if rape has been around since the "dawn of time," it must be natural and therefore normal and acceptable. Tiger's attempt to dismiss anti-rape efforts as merely the product of a "trend" is an attempt to erase debate on rape altogether by juxtaposing anti-rape discourses with the authoritative discourses of science. Likewise, the assertion that rape is merely a product of "different goals" establishes rape as a nonissue. It naturalizes rape through an assumption that the rapist's notions of rape are definitive, and that the horror of acquaintance rape comes from the naming alone. As women's narratives of rape demonstrate, this is not the case. . . .

[Backlash proponents endow rapists] with the authority to equate consent with failure to successfully resist rape.

[Another] way in which acquaintance rape is erased is through the denial of the female voice. The authority of the female voice is undermined when nonverbal "cues," which women supposedly emit, are considered to be more valid than what women say. Here, the "no doesn't really mean no" myth surfaces. Those who do not consider women's voices to be legitimate insist that it is OK to ignore a woman's words in favor of these "cues." By erasing women's words, backlash proponents can deny that acquaintance rape is really rape. An important consequence of the erasure of women's words is that it allows any aspect of a woman's behavior to be read as consent to any sexual act, regardless of her verbal communication. This makes it easy for lawyers, jurors, and rapists to deny that a rape has occurred. It also makes it virtually impossible for a woman to press charges for anything other than a violent stranger rape and difficult to press charges even in the case of a violent stranger rape. Timothy Beneke notes that this kind of erasure is an important part of victim blaming. He argues, "In all cases where a woman is said to have asked for it, her appearance and behavior are taken as a form of speech . . . the woman's actions . . . are given greater emphasis than her words."

An example of this form of erasure appears in a 1991 *Time* article. In "When Is It Rape?" the writer describes a rape case that was dropped due to lack of evidence because, as the victim said, "Who's gonna believe me? I had a man in my hotel room after midnight," despite her attacker's admission that he heard her say no. This is an obvious case of ignoring (erasing) the woman's voice in favor of irrelevant nonverbal cues. This particular rape case was dropped despite the fact that the man acknowledged that the woman had verbally refused consent. She said, "He says he didn't know that I meant no. He didn't feel he'd raped me." Clearly, in this case and others like it, the woman's consent or nonconsent is erased, allowing the rapist to define what rape is. College students are frequently quoted in backlash articles denying the validity of the female voice. One student said, "[If you're drunk and she] says no sometime later, even in the middle of the act, there still may be some kind of violation, but it's not the same thing. It's not rape. If you don't hear her say no, if she's playing around with you—oh, I could get squashed for saying it—there is an element of say no, mean yes." Here, female autonomy and the issue of consent are erased. The student's choice of words is telling: "If you don't hear her say no" suggests that the rapist's *hearing* nonconsent is what matters, not what the woman actually says. The student's statement that "there is an element of say no, mean yes," suggests that "hearing" consent has less to do with auditory perception than with his judgment of what (and *if*) women's words really mean. According to this logic, women have no right to judge whether a rape has occurred, since their refusal or consent is entirely superfluous. The erasure tactic denies women the power to define rape in general and denies women the authority to name rape even when it happens to them.

Reversal

The second tactic used in backlash discourse is reversal. The two main reversal tactics are

- Placing the responsibility for all manifestations of sexuality, including rape, on women (victim blaming)
- Defining consent-based definitions of rape as repressive to women

Reversal comprises the misappropriation of blame, responsibility, and victim status. According to the rhetoric of reversal, women cause rape. Moreover, reversal implies that consensual sex and consent-based definitions of rape are repressive to women, implying that rape itself is not harmful, only naming it is. Thus, the rapist is the true victim. He is victimized by women who impinge upon his exclusive right to determine what sex and rape are.

The first part of reversal is the placement of the responsibility for all sexuality, including rape, on women. Diana Russell summarizes this phenomenon in *The Politics of Rape:* "Women often take responsibility when men treat them as prey. This isn't just an odd female quirk. The attitude is deeply entrenched in the thinking of men, as well. Women are taught to make themselves attractive to men. Those who don't are ignored by men or incur their displeasure. But if they become victims of sexual assault, they are immediately suspected of collusion. No man is ever guilty. If he did something bad, it must have been invited." The idea that rape is more justifiable if a woman does not know, or adhere to, "the rules" is also a part of this tactic. Reversal tells us that women who "should have known better" than to let a man into their home, to wear a certain outfit, or to have sex outside of marriage are responsible for rape by men. Holding women to special rules, such as *Don't go out alone at night*, is blatant reversal, especially when her "transgression" is used to divert blame from the rapist, or when a woman who breaks these rules is viewed as inviting rape. As Beneke puts it, "If a woman trusts a man and goes to his apartment . . . or goes out on a date and is raped, she's a dupe and deserves what she gets. 'He didn't *really* rape her' goes the mentality—'he merely took advantage of her.'" By breaking the rules, women lose all of the "protection" afforded women by patriarchal culture (defense of her virtue, integrity, and so on). Women who break the rules are therefore rendered unrapeable. By unrapeable I do not mean that women who break the rules are safe from rape, but that their "misbehavior" is taken as unconditional and unlimited consent not only to sex but also to physical violence and other forms of abuse.

The term acquaintance rape allows women to name their rape experiences and get on with the recovery process.

The reversal of blame often appears in backlash discourse as the displacement of blame for rapes away from the men who rape. . . . *Newsweek* joins the protest against holding men responsible for rape with the comment "Thanks to nature, he's got the weapon," suggesting that rape is an inevitable, natural fact, and that men are the victims of anti-rape discourse because they have penises. With this statement the author ignores that fact that women *are* the usual victims of rape and men are the usual perpetrators, while using the same fact to naturalize rape. The logical implication of assertions that men are not responsible for rape is that women are responsible for it and that nonconsensual sex is "natural" and so there is nothing to be responsible *for*. As Roiphe suggests, if women are responsible for causing nonconsensual sex, it isn't really rape at all. "If we assume that women are not all helpless and naive, then they should be held responsible for their choice to drink or take drugs. If a woman's 'judgment is impaired' and she has sex, it isn't necessarily always the man's fault; it isn't necessarily always rape." First, it is important to mention that no one ever suggested that all sex when one partner's "judgment is impaired" is rape. The issue in determining if a rape occurred is whether the sex was consensual. Clearly, a person who is unconscious is unable to consent to sex. I doubt that any reasonable person would confuse an unconscious person's failure to refuse consent or resist rape with consent itself. Roiphe suggests that women are merely confusing consensual sex with rape. By simultaneously suggesting that women are incapable of determining whether they consented to sex and asserting that women are completely responsible for preventing rape, Roiphe puts women in a double bind: one with no authority and total responsibility, not just for their own actions, but for men's actions as well. The flip side of this is that men are absolved of responsibility for rape, and rapists are endowed with the authority to equate consent with failure to successfully resist rape. . . .

The second reversal tactic is the assertion that consent-based definitions of rape are repressive to women. Roiphe writes, "Let's not reinforce the images that oppress us, that label us victims, that deny our own agency and intelligence, as strong and sensual, as autonomous, pleasure seeking, sexual beings." What Roiphe implies is that merely discussing acquaintance rape does all of these things. According to Roiphe, talking about acquaintance rape, educating students about occurrence rates, and speaking out about rape is more oppressive than rape itself. Unfortunately, ignoring the reality of acquaintance rape does not make it go away. As women's rape narratives illustrate, language is very important to rape victims not because it *makes* them victims, but because it allows them to name a rape experience in a way that makes sense to them and to others. By definition, nonconsensual sex is not liberating or pleasurable for women. Pretending that it is forces women to seek sexual pleasure on someone else's terms and denies them both sexual agency and autonomy. . . .

The rejection of consent-based definitions of rape by the mainstream *Time, Newsweek,* and *New York Times* parallels right-wing sentiments about acquaintance rape. The *National Review* quotes Neil Gilbert, who has never conducted any original scientific research on rape, as a sociologist who has nonetheless made a "scrupulous analysis" of "this theory" and the "phantom 'epidemic of sexual assault' to which it has led." The "theory" in question is actually not theory at all, but the results of several studies on the incidence of rape. The *National Review* endorses Gilbert's statement that under consent-based definitions of rape, "the kaleidoscope of intimate discourse—passion, emotional turmoil, entreaties, flirtation, provocation, demureness—must give way to cool-headed contractual sex: 'Will you do it, yes or no? Please sign on the line below.'" The message is the same in *Time, Newsweek,* and the *New York Times. Time* says, "At the extreme, sexual relations come to resemble major surgery, requiring a signed consent form. . . . *Newsweek* equates acquaintance rape with "romantic disappointment" and "bad sex," asserting that "Everyone had bad sex back then [in the early seventies] and, to hear them tell, survived just fine."

Consent-based definitions of rape [concede] . . . the authority to consent to or refuse sex to individual women.

The problem is that women have never survived rape "just fine." Without the term acquaintance rape, women *couldn't* name their experiences for what they were: *rape* experiences. In fact, to hear them tell it, women have long been highly aware of the inadequacy of the language surrounding rape. Meg Nugent, who was raped by an acquaintance in

1976, says that she may not have identified what happened to her as rape then, but it was still a "terrifying experience," and it was still rape. Despite the fact that she was drugged and raped by her date, Nugent said, "I had to have outside confirmation to recognize that it was rape." The discussion of acquaintance rape in Robin Warshaw's *I Never Called It Rape* was the outside confirmation that allowed her to identify the incident as really rape. The term acquaintance rape made it directly possible for her to name, understand, and communicate about her rape experience for what it was. Thus, despite *Time*'s attempts to trivialize acquaintance rape as a figment of the overactive imaginations of victimhood-inducing feminists, the term acquaintance rape allows women to name their rape experiences and get on with the recovery process, a necessity that, to the detriment of women, was previously denied.

False polarization

False polarization is the creation and maintenance of artificial divisions between things that are not inherently opposite. In backlash discourse, this tactic works by means of a differentiation between "rape" and "Rape." This includes decisively distinguishing rapists from regular men, and distinguishing "rapeable" women from "normal" women. As I mentioned above, attempts to limit the use of the word rape to the description of stereotypical Rapes are part of backlash efforts to keep acquaintance rape from becoming part of the cultural vocabulary. It is a form of erasure as well as an example of false polarization. The division between rape and Rape is an important one. It serves to limit the concept of rape to extremely violent rapes by strangers. This kind of rape represents the minority of actual rape cases. The false polarization of rape and Rape discourages women who are raped by acquaintances, boyfriends, or husbands from reporting the rape, or even calling it what it is. False polarization is used to reinforce rape myths at the expense of effectively addressing the realities of sexual assault.

Time creates a distinction between Rape and rape by commenting that a student named Ginny Rayfield "was really raped when she was 16," as opposed to other women quoted in the same article, who apparently merely thought they had been raped. Katie Roiphe also has definite ideas about what rape is and is not. She expresses indignation that women dare to name acquaintance rape 'rape,' writing, "While real women get battered, while real mothers need day care, certain feminists are busy turning rape into fiction." In her article in the *New York Times Magazine*, Roiphe reveals her definition of real Rape: "It's hard to watch the solemn faces of young Bosnian girls, their words haltingly translated, as they tell of brutal rapes; or to read accounts of a suburban teen-ager raped and beaten while walking home from a shopping mall." Roiphe's idea of Rape is as stereotyped as can be, involving brutality, beatings, innocent young victims, foreigners, and strangers. Roiphe rejects the notion that consent divides rape from sex, writing, "It [a consent-based definition of rape] is measuring her word against his in a realm where words barely exist. There is a gray area in which one person's rape may be another's bad night." *Newsweek* agrees. A 1993 *Newsweek* article says, "Rape and sexual harassment are real. But between crime and sexual bliss are some cloudy waters." True, the scarcity of vocabulary surrounding rape does indeed create some "cloudy waters." Backlash writing suggests that this cloudiness in inevitable, and best left alone. However, what consent-based definitions of rape do is attempt to clear up this cloudiness by conceding the authority to consent to or refuse sex to individual women. This represents a radical reversal of power relative to context-based definitions of rape.

By limiting the use of the word 'rape' to the description of violent assaults perpetrated by a stranger, the majority of rapes are designated *not* rape and are defined as a lesser offense. This limitation is important because it labels rape as a freak occurrence—something perpetrated by a few crazy or sick men. It also falsely and decisively divides the rapist from "normal" men. The implication of such a division is that "regular" guys don't rape. This assumption reinforces women's fears of not being believed about having been raped by someone they know, and their feelings of guilt about not having identified him as a rapist prior to the rape. This polarization suggests that men who can get a date, or are attractive or popular, couldn't possibly rape—they are too normal. *Time* quotes a student who was accused of rape, and "angry and hurt" at the charges, saying, "Rape is what you read about in the *New York Post* about 17 little boys raping a jogger in Central Park." Clearly, under that definition, he could never do anything remotely resembling rape, even though he acknowledges that the woman who accused him of rape did not consent, and was "very drunk." The false polarization of rapists and normal men (and Rape and rape) also capitalizes on differences that are already culturally loaded, such as race and class. For example, *Time* recounts one woman's story of how the race of her assailant made it a Rape in the eyes of the police. "The first thing the Boston police asked was whether it was a black guy," she said. "So, you were really raped," was their reaction upon hearing that it was.

In addition to distorting the picture of who rapes, the false polarization between Rape and rape distorts the image of who gets raped. Under the stereotypical Rape definition, the women who get raped are usually those who don't play by the rules: women who go out after dark alone, women who hitchhike, women who dress "provocatively." This polarization serves to assure ordinary women that they can't be raped as long as they are careful. It also stigmatizes all rape victims in accordance with the idea that women who are raped are really just getting what they asked for. Limiting the use of the word rape to "Real Rape" sends the message that nonconsensual sex is acceptable unless it is especially violent and with a stranger. Of course, assurances based on myths are empty. Women are most often raped by someone they know.

Divide and conquer

The last tactic Daly names is divide and conquer. This tactic is an attempt to discredit efforts to fight acquaintance rape by suggesting that such efforts are the work of an overzealous fringe of "radical feminists" that most women, and even some feminists, oppose. By using this tactic, backlash discourses divert attention away from what anti-acquaintance rape efforts are fighting for and against. Anti-acquaintance rape efforts work to promote equality by authorizing women to determine whether they consented to a specific sexual act. One objective of this work is to hold men accountable for their actions when they choose to disregard that authority. Thus, anti-acquaintance rape efforts oppose the status quo that suggests that a variety of circumstances can mitigate a woman's right to refuse sex. Divide-and-conquer rhetoric creates the illusion that the only thing feminists are fighting is other women. The divide-and-conquer tactic obscures sexism and the problems caused by it, and it impedes efforts to address issues such as rape by persistently changing the subject. . . .

"Acquaintance rape" is a necessary term

Language is central to our individual attempts to understand and communicate our experiences. The availability of adequate vocabulary with which to enunciate our experiences is crucial to our constructions of ourselves and our understanding of the world in which we live. Since discourse, knowledge, and power are so closely interrelated, language is a site of contest. Dominant discourses are established in part by the inclusion, and exclusion, of specific words in the cultural vocabulary. The interjection of terms from subjugated discourses into dominant ones can effect significant changes to the existing episteme or horizon of meaning. As a result, changes in the cultural vocabulary can have a powerful impact on both the way in which we conceptualize our experiences and the conditions in which we live. . . . Discourses about rape are attempts to delineate which sexual behaviors are normal and which are deviant. Oppositional possibilities for changing rape-related language and ideas exist because "dominant meaning can be contested, alternative meanings confirmed." These possibilities include the potential to ratify a consent-based concept of rape, authorizing women to consent or refuse to engage in specific sexual acts.

As I argued earlier, women's statements about the rapes they have experienced illustrate the necessity for the term acquaintance rape. Backlash discourse on acquaintance rape is potentially damaging to women, since it stigmatizes the term acquaintance rape. Stigmatizing the term could effectively remove acquaintance rape from the cultural vocabulary, despite its usefulness, by designating it a product of sexual correctness. The erasure of acquaintance rape through sexual correctness rhetoric is an attempt to silence discourse on rape and contiguous issues, including gender roles and sexual norms. By learning to read rape discourses through a feminist lens, guided by the categories Daly names, women can maintain the usefulness of the term acquaintance rape despite backlash efforts. Identifying erasure, reversal, false polarization, and divide and conquer as backlash tactics provides an opportunity for undertaking oppositional readings of popular discourses on rape. Most important, this methodology may also be applied to other areas of discourse, facilitating oppositional readings of discourses on many issues across various forms of media.

5

Feminist Research Exaggerates the Prevalence of Acquaintance Rape

Neil Gilbert

Neil Gilbert is a professor of social welfare at the University of California at Berkeley and coauthor of Protecting Young Children from Sexual Abuse.

A study conducted by Mary Koss in 1985 is often cited by feminist groups in support of their claims that over half of all college women will be raped over four years, and more than one-quarter of them will be victimized twice. However, this study is flawed: Most of the women Koss labeled as victims of rape did not interpret their experiences as rape, and many continued sexual relationships with their supposed rapists. In addition, Koss offers unconvincing explanations, such as "self-blame," for the vast disparity that exists between her findings and the small numbers of rapes that are reported to college authorities. This flawed study is an example of advocacy research—playing fast and loose with the facts to persuade the public and policy makers that a problem is vastly larger than it really is.

According to the alarming accounts of sexual assault by certain feminist groups, about one out of every two women will be a victim of rape or attempted rape an average of twice in her life, one-third will have been sexually abused as children, and many more will suffer other forms of sexual molestation. These claims are based on figures from several studies, among which the *Ms.* Magazine Campus Project on Sexual Assault, directed by Mary Koss, [is one of the] . . . most widely disseminated and most frequently cited. . . .

[The study was] funded by the National Institute of Mental Health, giving [it] . . . the imprimatur of endorsement by a respected federal agency. Often quoted in newspapers and journals, on television, and during the 1991 Senate hearings on sexual assault, the findings from [this

Neil Gilbert, "Realities and Mythologies of Rape," *Society*, vol. 35, January/February 1998, pp. 356–62. Copyright © 1998 by Transaction Publishers. Reproduced by permission.

study] have gained a certain degree of authority by process of repetition. Most of the time, however, those who cite the research findings take them at face value without an understanding of where the numbers come from or what they represent.

Prefaced by sophisticated discussions of the intricate research methods employed, the findings are presented in a blizzard of data, supported by a few convincing cases and numerous references to lesser known studies. But footnotes do not a scholar make, and the value of quantitative findings depends upon how accurately the research variables are measured, how well the sample is drawn, and the analysis of the data. Despite the respected funding source, frequent media acknowledgment, and an aura of scientific respectability, a close examination of the two most prominent studies on rape reveals serious flaws that cast grave doubt on their credibility.

The 1985 *Ms.* study directed by Koss surveyed 6159 students at thirty-two colleges. As Koss operationally defines the problem, 27 percent of the female college students in her study had been victims of rape (15 percent) or attempted rape (12 percent) an average of two times between the ages of fourteen and twenty-one. Using the same survey questions, which she claims represent a strict legal description of the crime, Koss calculates that during a twelve-month period 16.6 percent of all college women were victims of rape or attempted rape and that more than one-half of these victims were assaulted twice. If victimization continued at this annual rate over four years, one would expect well over half of all college women to suffer an incident of rape or attempted rape during that period, and more than one-quarter of them to be victimized twice.

A notable discrepancy exists between Koss's definition of rape and the way most women she labeled as victims interpreted their experiences.

There are several reasons for serious researchers to question the magnitude of sexual assault conveyed by the *Ms.* findings. To begin with, a notable discrepancy exists between Koss's definition of rape and the way most women she labeled as victims interpreted their experiences. When asked directly, 73 percent of the students whom Koss categorized as victims of rape did not think that they had been raped. This discrepancy is underscored by the subsequent behavior of a high proportion of identified victims, forty-two percent of whom had sex again with the man who supposedly raped them. Of those categorized as victims of attempted rape, 35 percent later had sex with their purported offender.

Rape and attempted rape were operationally defined in the *Ms.* study by five questions, three of which referred to the threat or use of "some degree of physical force." The other two questions, however, asked: "Have you had a man attempt sexual intercourse (get on top of you, attempt to insert his penis) when you didn't want to by giving you alcohol or drugs, but intercourse did not occur? Have you had sexual intercourse when you didn't want to because a man gave you alcohol or drugs?" Forty-four percent of all the women identified as victims of rape and attempted rape in the previous year were so labeled because they responded positively to these awkward and vaguely worded questions. What does having sex "because" a man gives you drugs or alcohol signify? A positive response does not indicate whether duress, intoxication, force, or the threat of force were present; whether the woman's judgment or control were substantially impaired; or whether the man purposely got the woman drunk to prevent her from resisting his sexual advances. It could mean that a woman was trading sex for drugs or that a few drinks lowered the respondent's inhibitions and she consented to an act she later regretted. Koss assumes that a positive answer signifies the respondent engaged in sexual intercourse against her will because she was intoxicated to the point of being unable to deny consent (and that the man had administered the alcohol for this purpose). While the item could have been clearly worded to denote "intentional incapacitation of the victim," as the question stands it would require a mind reader to detect whether an affirmative response corresponds to a legal definition of rape.

A vast disparity exists between [Koss's] study findings and the rates of rape . . . that come to the attention of various authorities on college campuses.

Finally, a vast disparity exists between the *Ms.* study findings and the rates of rape and attempted rape that come to the attention of various authorities on college campuses. The number of rapes formally reported to the police on major college campuses is remarkably low—two to five incidents a year in schools with thousands of women. It is generally agreed that many rape victims do not report their ordeal because of the embarrassment and frequently callous treatment at the hands of the police. Over the last decade, however, rape crisis counselling and supportive services have been established on most major campuses. Highly sensitive to the social and psychological violations of rape, these services offer a sympathetic environment in which victims may obtain assistance without having to make an official report to the police. While these services usually minister to more victims than report to the local police, the numbers remain conspicuously low compared to the incidence of rape and attempted rape on college campuses as Koss defines the problem.

Inconsistent data

Applying Koss's finding of an annual incidence rate of 166 in 1000 women (each victimized an average of 1.5 times) to the population of 14,000 female students at the University of California at Berkeley in 1990, for example, one would expect about 2000 women to have experienced 3000 rapes or attempted rapes in that year. On the Berkeley campus, two rapes were reported to the police in 1990, and between forty and eighty students sought assistance from the campus rape counselling service. While this represents a serious problem, its dimensions (three to six cases in 1000) are a fraction of those (166 cases in 1000) claimed by the *Ms.* study.

What accounts for these discrepancies? Koss offers several explanations, some of which appear to derive from new data or additional analysis. Therefore it is important to distinguish between the data originally reported in 1987 and 1988 and later versions of the findings. The findings from the *Ms.* study were originally described in three articles, one by Koss and two co-authors in a 1987 issue of the *Journal of Consulting and Clinical Psychology*, the second (an expanded version of this article) authored by Koss as a chapter in the 1988 book, *Rape and Sexual Assault* (edited by Ann Burgess), and the third by Koss and three co-authors in a 1988 issue of the *Psychology of Women Quarterly*. Also published in 1988 was Robin Warshaw's book, *I Never Called It Rape: The Ms. Report on Recognizing, Fighting, and Surviving Date and Acquaintance Rape*, with an afterward by Koss describing the research methods used in the *Ms.* project on which the book was based.

It is hard to imagine that . . . college women . . . are unable to judge if a sexual encounter is consensual.

Two articles reported that only 27 percent of the students whom Koss classified as rape victims believed they had been raped. The third article in the *Psychology of Women Quarterly* (1988) provided additional data on how all these supposed victims labeled their experience. The findings reported here indicate that: 1) eleven percent of the students said they "don't feel victimized"; 2) forty-nine percent labeled the experience "miscommunication"; 3) fourteen percent labeled it "crime, but not rape"; and 4) twenty-seven percent said it was "rape."

Although there was no indication that other data might have been available on this question, three years later a surprisingly different distribution of responses is put forth. In answer to questions raised about the fact that most victims did not think they had been raped, Koss reported in the *Los Angeles Daily Journal* (July 17, 1991) that the students labeled as victims viewed the incident as follows: "One-quarter thought it was rape, one-quarter thought it was some kind of crime but did not believe it qualified as rape, one-quarter thought it was sexual abuse but did not think it qualified as a crime, and one-quarter did not feel victimized."

In a later paper, "Rape on Campus: Facing the Facts," the gist of these new findings was revised, with Koss recounting: "One-quarter thought it was some kind of crime, but did not realize it qualified as rape; one-quarter thought it was serious sexual abuse, but did not know it qualified as a crime."

These inconsistencies in the reported findings aside, the additional data are difficult to interpret. If one-quarter thought their incidents involved a crime, but not rape, what kind of crime did they have in mind? Were they referring to illegal activity at the time such as drinking underage or taking drugs? Despite Koss's elaboration on the data originally reported, at least one version of the findings reveal that 60 percent of the students either did not feel victimized or thought the incident was a case of miscommunication. Although in the second version many more students assessed the sexual encounter in negative terms, the fact remains that 73 percent did not think they were raped.

Concerning the 42 percent of purported victims who had sex afterwards with their supposed assailants, again new data appear to have surfaced. Describing these findings in her chapter in *Rape and Sexual Assault*, Koss notes: "Surprisingly, 42 percent of the women indicated that they had sex again with the offender on a later occasion, but it is not known if this was forced or voluntary; most relationships (87%) did eventually break up subsequent to the victimization." Three years later, in a letter to the *Wall Street Journal* (July 25, 1991), Koss is no longer surprised by this finding and evidently has new information revealing that when the students had sex again with the offenders on a later occasion they were raped a second time and that the relationship broke up not "eventually" (as do most college relationships), but immediately after the second rape.

Referring to this group's behavior, Koss explains: "Many victims reacted to the first rape with self-blame and thought that if they tried harder to be clear they could influence the man's behavior. Only after the second rape did they realize the problem was the man, not themselves. Afterwards, 87 percent of the women ended the relationship with the man who raped them." Koss also suggests that since many students were sexually inexperienced, they "lacked familiarity with what consensual intercourse should be like."

These explanations are not entirely convincing. It is hard to imagine that many twenty-one year old college women, even if sexually inexperienced, are unable to judge if a sexual encounter is consensual. As for the victims blaming themselves and believing they might influence the man's behavior if they tried harder the second time, Koss offers no data from her survey to substantiate this reasoning. Although research indicates that victims of rape tend to blame themselves, there is no evidence that this induces them to have sex again with their assailant. One might note that there are cases of battered wives who stay on with their husbands under insufferable circumstances. But it is not apparent that the battered-wife syndrome applies to a large proportion of female college students.

Room for misinterpretation

With regard to the operational definition of rape used in the *Ms.* study and described in the earlier reports, Koss continues to claim that the study measures the act of "rape legally defined as penetration against consent through the use of force, or when the victim was purposely incapacitated with alcohol or other drugs." No explanation is offered for how the researcher detects the "intentional incapacitation of the victim" from affirmative answers to questions such as: "Did you have unwanted sex because a man gave you alcohol?" Although these responses account for about 40 percent of the incidents classified as rape and attempted rape, when describing the study to the Senate Judiciary Committee and in other writings, Koss's examples of typical items used to define rape do not include these questions.

Reviewing the research methodology for the *Ms.* survey in *Rape and Sexual Assault* (1988) and the *Journal of Consulting and Clinical Psychology* (1987), Koss explains that reliability and validity studies conducted in 1985 on the ten-item Sexual Experience Survey (SES) instrument showed that few of the female respondents misinterpreted the questions on rape.

A serious question arises, however, whether the validity study cited by Koss was conducted on the version of the SES instrument that was actually used in the *Ms.* survey or on the original version of this instrument, which differed significantly from the one the *Ms.* findings are based on. The Sexual Experience Survey instrument originally designed by Koss and Oros, and reported on in a 1982 issue of the *Journal of Consulting and Clinical Psychology* contained none of the questions dealing with rape or attempted rape "because a man gave you alcohol or drugs."

In 1985, Koss and Gidycz reported (again in *Consulting and Clinical Psychology*) on the assessment of this instrument's validity, which they said indicates that: "To explore the veracity of the self-reported sexual experiences, the Sexual Experiences Survey (original wording) was administered to approximately 4000 students." Although Koss cites this report as evidence of the *Ms.* study instrument's validity, if the SES as originally worded was used, it is not at all clear that the assessment of validity included the vague items on "intentional incapacitation," which were absent from the original version of the SES instrument.

Elaborate research methods are employed . . . to persuade the public and policy-makers that a problem is vastly larger than commonly recognized.

Finally, the vast discrepancy between *Ms.* study figures and the number of students who generally seek rape counselling or report incidents of rape to authorities on college campuses is accounted for by the assertion that most college women who are sexually violated by an acquaintance do not recognize themselves as victims of rape. According to Koss, "many people do not realize that legal definitions of rape make no distinctions about the relationship between victim and offender." Findings from the Bureau of Justice Statistics suggest that the crime of being raped by an acquaintance may not be all that difficult to comprehend; in recent years 33 to 45 percent of the women who said they were raped identified their assailant as an acquaintance.

In support of the *Ms.* project findings, Koss invokes additional studies as sources of independent verification. Some of these use different definitions of forced sexual behavior (including verbal persuasion and psychological coercion) and involve samples too small or nonrepresentative for serious estimates of the size of the problem. Others are referred to without explanation or critical examination. For example, Koss cites Yegidis's findings in the *Journal of Sex Education and Therapy* (1986), which show a prevalence rate of rape for college students in the range reported by the *Ms.* study, as supportive evidence. But Yegidis defined rape as forced oral sex or intercourse, where the use of "force" included verbal persuasion. As she explains: "This study showed that most of the sexual encounters were forced through verbal persuasion—protestations by the male to 'go further' because of sexual need, arousal, or love." According to this definition, the conventional script of nagging and pleading "everyone does it," "if you really loved me, you'd do it," "I need it," "you will like it," is transformed into a version of rape.

Claiming that the *Ms.* survey's estimates of rape prevalence "are well-replicated in other studies," Koss refers to Craig's discerning review of the literature to confirm the consistency of prevalence data on college students. This is a curious citation, since Craig in fact is of a different opinion. Analyzing the problems of definition in *Clinical Psychology Review* (1990), she notes that they "vary from use of force to threat of force, to use of manipulative tactics such as falsely professing love, threatening to leave the woman stranded, or attempting to intoxicate the woman." Even when studies use the same general definitions, their authors often develop idiosyncratic measures to operationalize the terms. All of this leads Craig to conclude "that this lack of consistency limits the comparability of studies and makes replication of results difficult." . . .

The politics of advocacy research

The *Ms.* study by Koss [is a] highly sophisticated example of advocacy research. Elaborate research methods are employed under the guise of social science, to persuade the public and policy-makers that a problem is vastly larger than commonly recognized. This is done in several ways: 1) by measuring a problem so broadly that it forms a vessel into which almost any human difficulty can be poured; 2) by measuring a group highly impacted with the problem and then projecting the findings to society-at-large; 3) by asserting that a variety of smaller studies and reports with different problem definitions, methodologies of diverse quality, and varying results form a cumulative block of evidence in support of current findings; and 4) by a combination of the above.

Advocacy research is a phenomenon not unique to feminist studies of rape. It is practiced in a wide variety of substantive problem areas and supported by groups that, as Peter Rossi suggests, share an "ideological imperative," which maintains that findings politically acceptable to the advocacy community are more important than the quality of research from which they are derived. Playing fast and loose with the facts is justifiable in the service of a noble cause, just as is condemning or ignoring data and sentiments that challenge conventional wisdom. Denounced for expressing objectionable sentiments, for example, folk singer Holly Dunn's hit, "Maybe I Mean Yes—When I Say No" was clearly out of tune with the feminist mantra, "no means no." The controversy over these lyrics ignored Muehlenhard and Hollabaugh's inconvenient findings that 39 percent of the 610 college women they surveyed admitted to having said no to sexual advances when they really meant yes and fully intended to have their way.

Although advocacy studies do little to elevate the standards of social science research, they sometimes serve a useful purpose in bringing grave problems to public attention. No matter how it is measured, rape is a serious problem that creates an immense amount of human suffering. One might say that even if the rape research magnifies this problem in order to raise public consciousness, it is being done for a good cause, and in any case the difference is only a matter of degree. So why make an issue of the numbers?

The issue is not that advocacy studies simply overstate the incidence of legally defined rape, but the extent to which this occurs and what it means. After all, the difference between boiling and freezing is "only a matter of degree." The tremendous gap between estimates of rape and attempted rape that emerge from data collected annually by the Bureau of Justice Statistics (BJS) and the figures reported in advocacy studies have a critical bearing on our understanding of the issue at stake.

The BJS surveys, actually conducted by the Census Bureau, interview a random sample of about 62,000 households every six months. The confidentiality of responses is protected by federal law and response rates amount to 96 percent of eligible units. The interview schedule asks a series of screening questions such as: Did anyone threaten to beat you up or threaten you with a knife, gun, or some other weapon? Did anyone try to attack you in some other way? Did you call the police to report something that happened to you that you thought was a crime? Did anything happen to you which you thought was a crime, but you did not report to the police?

A positive response to any of these screening items is followed up with questions like: What actually happened? How were you threatened? How did the offender attack you? What injuries did you suffer? When, where did it happen, what did you do, and so forth.

Most men aren't rapists

As a guide to trends in sexual assault, the BJS data show that rates of rape and attempted rape declined by about 30 percent between 1978 and 1988. As for recent experience, BJS findings reveal that 1.2 women in 1000 over twelve years of age were victims of rape or attempted rape. This amounted to approximately 135,000 female victims in 1989. No trivial number, this annual figure translates into a lifetime prevalence rate of roughly 5 to 7 percent, which suggests that one woman out of fourteen is likely to experience rape or attempted rape sometime in her life. As do other victimization surveys, the BJS studies have problems of subject recall, definition, and measurement, which, as Koss and others have pointed out, lead to underestimation of the amount of sexual assault.

[There are] huge differences between federal [rape prevalence] estimates and advocacy research findings.

Assuming that the BJS survey underestimated the problem by 50 percent—that is, that it missed one out of every two cases of rape or attempted rape in the sample—the lifetime prevalence rate would rise to approximately 10 to 14 percent. Although an enormous level of sexual assault, at that rate the BJS estimates would still be dwarfed by the findings of Koss and [other] . . . studies, which suggest that one in two women will be victimized an average of twice in their life.

This brings us to the crux of the issue, that is, the huge differences between federal estimates and advocacy research findings have implications that go beyond matters of degree in measuring the size of the problem. If almost half of all women will suffer an average of two incidents of rape or attempted rape sometime in their lives, one is ineluctably driven to conclude that most men are rapists. "The truth that must be faced," according to [feminist researcher Diana] Russell, "is that this culture's notion of masculinity—particularly as it is applied to male sexuality—predisposes men to violence, to rape, to sexually harass, and to sexually abuse children."

To characterize [sexual miscommunication] . . . as rape trivializes the trauma and pain suffered by . . . the true victims of this crime.

In a similar vein, Koss claims that her findings support the view that sexual violence against women "rests squarely in the middle of what our culture defines as 'normal' interaction between men and women." Catherine MacKinnon, one of the leading feminists in the rape crisis movement, offers a vivid rendition of the theme that rape is a social disease afflicting most men. Writing in the *New York Times* (December 15, 1991), she advises that when men charged with the crime of rape come to trial, the court should ask "did this member of a group sexually trained to woman-hating aggression commit this particular act of woman-hating sexual aggression?"

Advocacy research not only promulgates the idea that most men are rapists, it provides a form of "scientific" legitimacy for promoting social programs and individual behaviors that act on this idea. When asked if college women should view every man they see as a potential rapist, a spokeswoman for the student health services at the University of California, Berkeley, told the *Oakland Tribune* (May 30, 1991), "I'm not sure that would be a negative thing." This echoes the instruction supplied in one of the most popular college guidebooks on how to prevent acquaintance rape. "Since you can't tell who has the potential for rape by simply looking," the manual warns, "be on your guard with every man."

These experts on date rape advise college women to take their own cars on dates or to have a back-up network of friends ready to pick them up, to stay sober, to go only to public places, to be assertive, to inform the man in advance what the sexual limits will be that evening, and to prepare for the worst by taking a course in self-defense beforehand. Separately, some of the instructions, such as staying sober, are certainly well advised. Collectively, however, this bundle of cautions transmits the unspoken message that dating men is a very dangerous undertaking.

Beyond seeking courses in self-defense, the implications drawn from advocacy research sometimes recommend more extreme measures. Last year, at a public lecture on "The Epidemic of Sexual Violence Against Women," Diana Russell was asked by a member of her largely feminist audience whether, in light of the ever-present danger, women should start carrying guns to protect themselves against men. Stating that personal armament was a good idea, but that women should probably take lessons to learn how to hit their target, Russell's response was greeted with loud applause.

Not all feminists, or members of the rape crisis movement, agree with the view that all men are predisposed to be rapists. Gillian Greensite, founder of the Rape Prevention Education program at the University of California, Santa Cruz, writes that the seriousness of this crime "is being undermined by the growing tendency of some feminists to label all heterosexual miscommunication and insensitivity as acquaintance rape." (One is reminded that 50 percent of the students whom Koss defined as victims of rape labelled their experience as "miscommunication.") This tendency, Greensite observes, "is already creating a climate of fear on campuses, straining relations between males and females."

Heightened confusion and strained relations between men and women are not the only dysfunctional consequences of advocacy research that inflates the incidence of rape to a level that indicts most men. According to Koss's data, rape is an act that most educated women do not recognize as such when it has happened to them, and after which almost half of the victims go back for more. To characterize this type of sexual encounter as rape trivializes the trauma and pain suffered by the many women who are true victims of this crime, and may ultimately make it more difficult to convict their assailants. By exaggerating the statistics on rape, advocacy research conveys an interpretation of the problem that advances neither mutual respect between the sexes nor reasonable dialogue about assaultive sexual behavior.

It is difficult to criticize advocacy research without giving the impression of caring less about the problem than those engaged in magnifying its size. But one may be deeply concerned about the problem of rape and still wish to see a fair and objective analysis of its dimensions. Advocacy studies have, in their fashion, rung the alarm. Before the rush to arms, a more precise reading of the data is required to draw an accurate bead on this problem and attack it successfully.

6

Feminist Research Does Not Exaggerate the Prevalence of Acquaintance Rape

Martin D. Schwartz and Molly S. Leggett

Martin D. Schwartz is a professor of sociology at Ohio University and coauthor of Sexual Assault on the College Campus *and* Researching Sexual Violence Against Women. *Molly S. Leggett is a corrections classification specialist in the Ohio Department of Rehabilitation and Corrections.*

Researcher Mary Koss's frequently cited 1985 rape study has come under attack by U.S. conservatives who maintain that it grossly exaggerates the number of acquaintance rapes on college campuses. Critics contend that Koss inflates her rape numbers by counting regretable, psychologically harmless sexual encounters caused by intoxication as rape. They insist that only women physically forced to have sex should be considered rape victims. These assertions are proven unfounded by new research. Women who were unable to consent to sex due to intoxication are even more likely than physically forced women to suffer emotional distress. The reason that many of these rapes go unreported is that, in a society that rewards men for sexual aggressiveness, women wrongly blame themselves for their victimization.

One of the primary props behind the commonly asserted claim that one in four college women has been the victim of rape or attempted rape is Mary Koss's carefully constructed national representative sample of college women. For this reason, this study has come under the most attack from U.S. conservatives. Sponsored by the *Ms.* Foundation, Koss and her colleagues surveyed 6,159 undergraduate women and men from coast to coast [in 1985]. Her findings have been commonly supported in other similar and replication studies.

Neil Gilbert, the primary advocate of the argument that there are not large numbers of acquaintance rapes on college campuses, argues that

Martin D. Schwartz and Molly S. Leggett, "Bad Dates or Emotional Trauma? The Aftermath of Campus Sexual Assault," *Violence Against Women*, vol. 5, March 1999, pp. 251–71. Copyright © 1999 by Sage Publications, Inc. Reproduced by permission.

Koss's one in four figure is due to the loose wording of her questions. He argues that the questions were not structured well enough to allow the conclusion that these women were raped. For example, he attacks as too broad Koss's questions that "referred to the threat or use of some degree of physical force" [in his 1992 article "The Phantom Epidemic of Sexual Assault"]. Because three of the five rape and attempted rape questions used this phrase, Gilbert contends that the questions were too vague and subject to a woman's interpretation. He further states that her other two questions pose a problem because they ask about sexual encounters when the man gave them drugs or alcohol. He is concerned that the woman would have no way of knowing if she was given drugs or alcohol to enable the man to have sex with her. Or, according to Gilbert, it is possible that the woman had a few too many drinks and then regretted the sex.

Tolerance for rape in intimate relationships is still widespread and . . . many educated college students freely blame the woman for [rape].

What Gilbert contends is that because these women often did not define their experiences as rape, rape must not be what happened. Researchers like Koss are making an issue out of sexual experiences that women simply engaged in but then regretted. Gilbert further goes on to suggest that these women would have at least talked to a rape crisis center had they remotely thought they had been raped. He believes that because rape crisis centers do not automatically report rapes to the authorities, any woman would feel safe about reporting the rape and discussing her experiences.

Generally, then, Gilbert's argument is that because these women did not report that they had been raped, then Koss and other similar researchers are using a different definition than the one in the criminal law—they are using the radical feminist critique. Gilbert suggests that because the women questioned were in college, they were too educated not to realize they had been raped. [In her 1993 book *The Morning After*,] Katie Roiphe, following in these footsteps, strongly advocates the belief that many women who cry "rape" simply had a bad experience that they regret. She states that in today's world, politically correct sex involves a yes, and a specific yes at that: a new standard pamphlet on acquaintance rape warns men that "hearing a clear sober 'yes' to the question 'Do you want to make love?' is very different from thinking, 'Well, she didn't say no.'"

She goes on to say that the *luxury* of unspoken consent has basically gone out the window, and that this is a sad reflection of today's world.

Another controversial area deals with the problem of sexual intercourse while the woman is too drunk or high to give consent. This is, of course, a particular problem on college campuses, where the use of alcohol is exceptionally high. The issue is whether a woman who has had too much to drink and is physically incapable of giving her consent has been raped or if she has simply not refused. It is a matter of calling it rape or consensual sex. But the law is clear in most jurisdictions that the crime of rape consists of sexual acts without a woman's consent, and that the act is rape if the woman is incapable of giving consent (unconscious, of low mental capacity, too intoxicated to give consent). If the woman is incapable of saying yes, the act is considered to be rape. Generally, case law on this subject is many decades old.

An important attack on Koss's work is that she used the definition found in the first-degree rape statute in Ohio, where she was working at the time. Ohio law requires a finding (for a first-degree conviction) that the aggressor gave the victim alcohol or drugs for the purpose of rendering her incapable of giving consent. It specifically excludes such events as sharing a bottle of wine in an attempt to create a romantic moment. Koss thus asked if a woman had ever had sexual intercourse when she did not want to because a man had given her alcohol or drugs. Interestingly, many critics strongly argue opposite interpretations on what women are capable of understanding. On one hand, they find it clear that college women are often not capable of understanding the Koss question as meaning that they had not given consent to the act of intercourse. Women, evidently, are confused by sexual intercourse in the context of alcohol, and do not even know when they have given consent or not. Yet, the same critics also find it impossible to believe the central point of Koss's findings—that educated college women would sometimes not know whether to use the term *rape* to describe what happened to them. College women, they argue, are clearly capable of knowing whether they gave consent.

There is no question that . . . a large number of rape victims blame themselves after being raped.

At any rate, in our study we tried to make the connection more clear by asking if the woman had sexual intercourse when she did not want to because she was unable to give her consent or stop the man because of being intoxicated or on drugs. This is an act that is without doubt a felony crime. The issue is clear. If Gilbert and Roiphe are correct, then rape researchers are counting events as rape when the women themselves are only arguing that they were a bit annoyed that they had sexual intercourse that night and sort of regretted doing it. Obviously, when compared with the tremendous trauma caused by rape, these would be trivial events. On the other hand, if rape researchers are correct, then these are indeed rapes.

Self-blame

The importance of these questions is that many women believe that if they are too intoxicated or drugged to say no, then they are to blame for the sexual assault. Tolerance for rape in intimate relationships is still widespread in the United States, and a great many educated college students freely blame the woman for an act of male aggression in a variety of circumstances. In general, women live in the same society and hear the same messages as men whether it is through the news media or friends. They engage in extensive self-blame, and in many cases are helped to engage in this self-blame by the reactions of important friends and intimates. There has not been much study of this question, but the few studies that have compared stranger rape victims with acquaintance rape victims have found more self-blame among the latter group. This is fully consistent with the various scenario studies asking college students whom they would blame if the occasion arose.

As critics have noted, some respondents in the Koss and similar studies do not claim that they are rape victims. It is not uncommon for women who have been attacked to be unable to fully understand that the incident that is bothering them is actually an event defined by criminal law as felony rape. However, this difficulty in putting a name to the event does not mean that they are unaffected by it. Robin Warshaw [author of the 1988 book *I Never Called It Rape*] discusses this trauma:

> [L]ike a stranger-rape victim, her [the acquaintance rape victim] confidence in the world has been upended; unlike a stranger-rape victim, few people will offer her sympathy due to social myths about acquaintance rape, the tendency to blame the victim.

She argues that many women cannot stop feeling guilty for the rape, as if they could or should have somehow stopped it. Victoria L. Pitts and Martin D. Schwartz's 1997 study ["Sexual Coercion in Dating Situations Among University Students"] of hidden rape victims shows that victim blame serves to create situations where victims are "internalizing what others are telling them about who is at fault for unwanted, nonconsensual intercourse (whether it be a generalized, societal other, or the specific peers with whom they discuss their experience)." Here, the finding was that rape survivors who had close friends who told them that they were at fault did not believe that they had been raped. Rape survivors who had friends who told them they were not to blame all believed that they were raped. The basic finding was that whether women said they had been raped or not depended more on the reactions of their friends than any other issue. This is especially important in light of such findings as Robert C. Davis and Ellen Brickman that rape victims are particularly likely to be the subject of unsupportive behavior from "significant others." This must be tied to Sarah E. Ullman's 1996 finding that women who were the subject of negative social reactions were clearly more likely to show increased psychological symptoms after the event. The net result of these studies is to show that self-blame is a serious issue for rape survivors.

Emotional effects

An area closely related to self-blame is how affected emotionally and psychologically the woman is after a sexual assault. As noted above, the reaction of her friends and the amount of self-blame she takes upon herself can be relevant to this distress. There is a reasonably large literature in psychology that divides the victims of sexual assault into two groups: stranger rape and acquaintance rape. In examining these women, researchers are typically unable to differentiate between the two groups in terms of later psychological symptoms. [In 1997,] P.A. Frazier and L.M. Seales found that "the overall trend is that stranger and acquaintance rape victims do not differ in terms of postrape distress and symptomatology." They found, however, that very little work had been done comparing acknowledged versus unacknowledged rape victims, and in their own work found very little difference in psychological distress between these two groups. Women who do not admit to themselves that they are rape victims are just as likely to suffer from psychological distress as those who name their experiences as *rape.*

Although these studies are directly relevant to the question here, they do not speak exactly to the question. Critics have claimed that women who engaged in unwanted sexual intercourse or other sexual acts while too intoxicated to give consent or protest were not as psychologically distressed as women who were the victims of rape by force. Many people on campus argue and even teach that "working out a yes" by getting a woman so drunk that she cannot protest is a reasonably legitimate behavior rather than a felony rape. In some communities, officials ranging from student judicial boards to local police and prosecutors refuse to define any acquaintance sexual victimization as a crime.

---

*In our version [of questions asked college women],
. . . it is clear the act was rape under virtually all
state statutes.*

Thus, a goal of this research was to investigate the claims of critics that women are not as affected by acquaintance rape as feminists claim, by looking directly at the differences between those women who were assaulted while drunk or high and those women who were forced into sexual intercourse or acts.

Hypothesis

It is an important part of backlash arguments that women who experience unwanted sexual intercourse because of intoxication are relatively unaffected by the sexual experience. The presumption is that women physically forced to have sex are the victims of "real rape," and that "real rape" victims are more emotionally distressed by what happened. Thus, the first hypothesis is: 1. The women who were raped due to intoxication are significantly less affected by the event than the women who were raped due to physical force.

Second, there is no question that an important psychological factor in rape is self-blame, and that a large number of rape victims blame themselves after being raped. However, it is an important argument of rape critics that intoxicated women in particular blame themselves for the sexual victimization. Thus, the second hypothesis. 2. The women raped because of alcohol or drugs blame themselves for the event more than do the women raped by physical force. Finally, Koss makes the argument that women whose experiences meet the legal definition of rape generally do not believe that they were raped; in her survey, only 27% of the women who were raped agreed with the word rape to describe their experience. Here, although we agree with Koss, we further specify that even fewer women who were raped because of intoxication will report that their experience was a rape. 3. The women who have been raped because of force will be more likely to label their experiences as rape than will women who had unwanted sex because they were too intoxicated to resist. If the critics are correct that rape researchers are inflating minor events into a moral panic, then it would seem likely that women who were physically forced into sexual intercourse would be the ones most likely to apply the label rape to the event that occurred. However, this argument would suggest that the confusion and self-blame involved in rape by intoxication will make it difficult for many of these victims to label what happened to them as rape.

Methods

In order to investigate some of these issues, we created a questionnaire using previously used surveys, but mainly Koss's 1985 Sexual Experience Survey (SES). We added open-ended questions at the end discussing the aftermath of the experience. Because most previous surveys had relied primarily on first- and second-year students, we decided to limit our sample entirely to seniors. In this way, we thought, we might be maximizing the amount of time available for sexual experiences while at college. The university used requires senior-year integrative classes. By sampling these classes, we obtained usable questionnaires from 388 females in 25 classes. Although data were simultaneously collected from men, in this study we used data only from the female respondents.

[More than 90 percent of] women raped because they were unable to give consent due to intoxication . . . claimed to be affected by the event.

The students were given a human subjects research consent form, which was read verbatim by the administrator, then signed, dated, and collected from each participating student. Each anonymous survey was completed in class and no extra credit was given. Participation was completely voluntary and students were informed verbally and in writing that they were free to stop answering questions at any time with no questions asked and no penalties. Only five females did not complete usable questionnaires. Given the criticisms that SES questions were loosely worded, we tightened up several questions to remove any misunderstanding. For example, as noted earlier, the SES question most attacked by Gilbert and Roiphe was "Have you had sexual intercourse when you didn't want to because a man gave you alcohol or drugs?" Critics complain that students might not know the difference between seduction and rape. In our version, we asked "Have you engaged in sexual intercourse when you didn't want to but were so intoxicated or under the influence of alcohol or drugs that you could not stop it or object?" In using such wording, it is clear that the reason the woman had sex with the man was because she was physically or mentally unable to resist. It is clear the act was rape under virtually all state statutes. We also eliminated questions asking women if they had agreed to sexual intercourse because of a man's overwhelming pressures and arguments.

Critics have also expressed concern that some rape researchers put into one global variable a variety of types of sexual assault and coercion. Both to speak to that criticism and also to see if the two types of victims under discussion here were different on our questions, we created a variable called *rapetype*. This variable divided attempted and completed rape into two categories: (a) rape (and attempted rape) while unable to give consent because of alcohol or drug intoxication, and (b) rape (or attempted rape) because the male used or threatened physical force. Included in the first category are attempted and completed intercourse due to intoxication, whereas the second category includes rape by force as well as sex acts (anal or oral intercourse, or penetration by objects other than the penis) due to physical force. Of course, as explained earlier, we did not use the word rape with the respondents: they were asked about behavior as described in the statute.

Self-blame was measured by a simple variable. Women who reported that they were the victims of events measured by rapetype were asked to report for the most serious event whether they blamed themselves for what happened, whether they blamed the man for what happened, or whether they blamed both themselves and the man. One woman said she did not know, and one woman said "nobody," and these were removed from the tables for statistical reasons.

Finally, the women in this survey who reported that they were the victims of an unwanted sexual experience were asked to self-report on how much they were psychologically and emotionally affected by that experience. We asked the women to categorize their response using the following choices:

1. It was not very important to me; I was not much affected.
2. It did not bother me for very long; I bounced back fairly quickly.
3. It affected me. I changed as a person (e.g., not as trusting, depressed, unhappy, or some other reaction).
4. It deeply affected me and caused emotional pain.

Findings

Of the 388 women who filled out the questionnaires in this survey, 65 reported that they were victims of an event that would under Ohio law be considered a felony rape. Thirty-five reported that they had been the victims of unwanted sexual intercourse when they were helpless to resist or stop the man, whereas 30 reported that they were overcome with force or a threat of force.

Because [many] women do not recognize their experience as rape the crimes do not get reported.

In Table 1, we see that of the women raped due to physical force, there were 16.7% who claimed to be unaffected versus only 5.7% of women victimized because of alcohol or drugs. In total, we see that of the women raped because they were unable to give consent due to intoxication, 94.2% claimed to be affected by the event versus 83.4% of the physically forced women. Furthermore, there were similar numbers of women affected or deeply affected by the experiences in each category. As Table 1 clearly shows, the overwhelming majority of women were affected in some way. Perhaps more important, there is no statistically significant difference in the reported emotional outcome between the two groups of women: one cannot say that women who were raped by force were more psychologically affected than those raped while intoxicated. Stated another way, these data do not support the first hypothesis prediction that women who were raped by intoxication were less likely to report psychological or emotional distress. Table 2 shows rapetype by whom the women blame for the event. Once again, it is the lack of statistical significance in this table that is interesting. It is perhaps not surprising, although it is saddening, that 79.3% of the women who were raped while intoxicated put all or part of the blame on themselves. All of these women were the victims of a felony crime, and all said specifically that the only reason that they had unwanted sexual intercourse was that they were unable to resist or fight back. What might be surprising to many is that 50% of the women raped by force or threat of force also took on some degree of self-blame. More specifically, we need to look only at those women who completely blamed themselves for what happened. It seems to fit many of the messages in society that slightly more than one fourth of all of the women raped while intoxicated completely blamed themselves for what happened. However, virtually one quarter of the women raped by force took on all of the blame also.

Table 1: Whether Women Were Affected by the Type of Assault

	Type of Rape		
How Affected	Alcohol	Physical Force	Total
Unaffected	5.7	16.7	10.8
Somewhat affected	51.4	26.7	40.0
Affected	31.4	36.7	33.8
Deeply affected	11.4	20.0	15.4
Total	53.8	46.2	100.0

NOTE: Total affected: alcohol = 94.2%, physical force = 83.4%.

Table 2: Whom the Women Blame by the Type of Assault

	Type of Rape		
Who to Blame	Alcohol	Physical Force	Total
Myself	27.6	22.7	25.5
Man	20.7	50.0	33.3
Both	51.7	27.3	41.2
Total	56.9	43.1	100.0

At the end of the questionnaire, removed from the other questions, we asked the simple question of whether the woman answering the survey had been raped since coming to college. What is important is that all of the 51 women who chose to answer this question had already stated in response to the questions used to develop Tables 1 and 2 that they had in fact been victims of rape since coming to college. However, Table 3, for the first time, introduces the use of the word rape. In other words, all of the women being asked if they had been raped had in fact been raped. Yet, in response to the question that specifically asked "Have you ever been raped," only 1 victim (3.3%) raped while too intoxicated to give consent answered affirmatively, and only 5 victims (23.8%) raped because of physical force said that they had. The latter figure generally agrees with Koss and numerous other researchers who have found that about 25% or so of rape victims label the event as rape. What is important in Table 3 is that what Koss called the problem of the "hidden rape victim" is much worse in the case of the woman raped while intoxicated. Hidden rape victims who do not define what happened to them as rape do not seek out the services of rape counselors, do not attend to various mental health services, and often do not understand why they are suffering from various symptoms of emotional pain. In a way, Gilbert is correct. He argued that if women thought that they were rape victims they would no doubt go to a rape crisis center in order to get help. Although his argument is that a lack of crisis center calls means that there is much less rape than feminists claim, the argument here is that these hidden rape victims do not seek care because they do not see that they are victims. They do not make this recognition because they live in a society that makes women responsible as gate-keepers for sexual relations, rewards men for sexual aggressiveness, and blames women for their own victimization. What we have found in this society is that a tremendous number of women engage in self-blame for being victimized by predatory rapists.

Table 3: Whether Woman Says She Was Raped, by Type of Assault

	Type of Rape		
Have Ever Been Raped	Alcohol	Physical Force	Total
Yes	3.3	23.8	11.8
No	96.7	76.2	88.2
Total	58.8	41.2	100.0

In total, 11.8% of all of the rape victims said that they had been raped. Recall that in Table 1, virtually all rape victims were emotionally or psychologically affected, and a majority was seriously affected. Yet, because these women do not recognize their experience as rape the crimes do not get reported, the rapists are not prosecuted, and the women do not receive victim services.

Discussion and conclusions

The first decision made in this study was to reject Hypothesis 1; there is no evidence that women raped due to intoxication were less affected emotionally than women who were raped by force. The numbers show that virtually all victims of rape are affected, regardless of the circumstances surrounding the act. Roiphe and other backlash theorists are wrong to assume that women who are too drunk to say no are unaffected by the rape. These women certainly feel the effects of such acts: Our study shows that only 5.7% did not claim to be affected. Again, this means that 94.3% were affected in some way, with 11.4% being deeply affected. This is a high percentage of women to be affected and not receive help. Virtually everyone who has done research in this field argues that the methodology we used is likely to be conservative in terms of eliciting admissions from women that they were victims of rape. Many women report on anonymous questionnaires that they have never told anyone of their experience, and it is at least logical to assume (if we cannot prove it) that some of these women would continue to keep their secret, even in an anonymous questionnaire.

Universities and colleges need to actively work to search out hidden [rape] victims.

The second hypothesis specifies that the women who were raped while intoxicated would blame themselves more than would women who were raped by force. This hypothesis was also rejected. Still, although the table did not reach statistical significance, it is instructive to look at the percentages in the table. As mentioned earlier, about one quarter of all rape victims blame themselves entirely. It is a very important commentary on the power of ideology and the nature of courtship patriarchy that women continue to blame themselves even when they are the victims of a rape accomplished through the use of force. Feminist theorists often argue that our society is one that accepts sexual assault as normative. If that is the case, it is no wonder that so many women are affected emotionally and psychologically by it, but still blame themselves and do not report it to the police. Pitts and Schwartz and Frazier and Seales discuss how self-blame leads to silence, meaning the rapes will not be reported to the police or campus security. To explain this, Koss developed the notion of hidden victims, noting that in her study only 5% of the rapes were reported to the police. Here, we found essentially the same thing. Of 43 women who answered this question, only 2 (4.7%) had reported their sexual assault to the police. Women generally do not report their victimization, in part because of self-blame and embarrassment.

Thus, if too many men act like they can force sexual intercourse on a woman any time they wish on college campuses and get away with it, it is because it is too often true. In fact, they can often act with impunity. When approximately 5% of victimized women are reporting even forcible rape, there is very little reason for a rapist to fear any consequences of his actions. Worse yet, too few campuses act with concern for the crimes that are reported. Some campuses are more concerned with covering up and hiding victimization than they are with helping victims. Others are committed to a nonadversarial justice system that requires the victim to act as prosecutor if she wishes any action to be taken. This burden may be more than a raped woman wishes to handle. Finally, many universities have other priorities. For example, the *New York Times* reported on one elite campus that did not take significant action against an admitted rapist, but did expel the friend of the rape victim, who sat with her during the proceedings, for being caught with an open container of beer.

Technically, our third hypothesis was confirmed. There is a statistically significant difference in that women who were raped by force or threat of force are more likely to classify their experience as rape than are women raped while intoxicated. The problem with this interpretation, however, is that it is only technically correct. Of the women whose experiences fit the definition of rape, only 11.8% classified their experience as rape, a finding consistent with other studies. In other words, although the hypothesis is correct, actually very few women of any experience labeled their experience as rape. The results of this study are simple enough. When the Koss SES survey's criticized questions are "tightened up," the percentage of women who report being victimized by sexual assaults remains high. At the same time, the strong tendency shown here is for women to commonly take the blame upon themselves, either fully or partially, for the behavior of male rapists and sexual aggressors. This continues to create hidden victims and to keep women from seeking the help they need. Unfortunately, this provides a lack of deterrence that makes it possible for current patterns of sexual assault to continue on the college campus. By moving the blame from the rapist to the victim, it even takes away the survivors' right to get mad about what happened to her. The implications of this study are clear. In the first place, rape programming on college campuses needs to center clearly on blame and self-blame. If women do not recognize that they have been involved in an assault, then they will not seek help. Clearly, those women who have been victimized by acquaintances in a situation without force but where they were too drunk to resist also are in need of various forms of support. Furthermore, another form of rape programming must be to educate people on how to react to friends who have survived an unwanted sexual experience. Clearly, those women who have supportive friends who help her direct blame externally are more likely to be in a position to seek counseling and other support.

Universities and colleges need to actively work to search out hidden victims. The fact that these women do not believe they have been raped, or that they are innocent of blame, does not mean that they are not in need of support services.

Finally, rape programmers need to take results such as the ones from this study strongly into account when developing methods of spending scarce resources. On many campuses today with very low stranger rape rates, student groups are demanding that all available funds be spent on escort patrols, blue light telephones, the removal of bushes, increased lighting, and increased police patrols. Although these measures can be very useful in reducing fear of rape, they have nothing to do with the most prevalent form of rape on campus. Blue light telephones will not help with a date, and it is unlikely that police will start to patrol fraternity houses and apartments. This study joins a number of others to argue that acquaintance rape, even if accomplished without force, has an effect on women's lives and should be a focus of campus task forces.

7

Cultural Messages Contribute to the Prevalence of Date Rape

Alyn Pearson

Alyn Pearson wrote the following viewpoint while attending Bard College in New York State. She was a member of Bard's Response to Rape and Associated Violence Education (BRAVE), a group that deals with rape and sexual assault within the college community.

American popular culture reinforces society's unspoken tolerance for date and acquaintance rape by depicting women as passive receptors of male aggression. Through magazines, television, and the movies, women are bombarded with the message that they must defer to the desires of men—pressure that too often translates into sexual assault. These powerful cultural signals make it difficult for women to say no to rape—commonly mislabeled "unwanted sex"—and leave them feeling afraid, ashamed, and depressed. Women must act with conviction and self-confidence in rejecting America's violent "rape culture."

Rape is the common cold of society. Although rape is much more serious than the common cold, the symptoms are the same. We have assimilated rape into our everyday culture much as we have the cold. Like the folklore surrounding the common cold, there is folklore about rape, like the notion that if a woman wears revealing clothing or goes to a bar alone, she is likely to "get raped." But in fact a woman is no more likely to be raped from these activities than from simply dating a man or being home alone.

The rape culture

There is a silence surrounding the recognition that we live in a cultural environment where rape is endemic but it is true. The rape culture is much like the poor sanitation conditions which led to typhoid—it pro-

Alyn Pearson, "Rape Culture: It's All Around Us," *Off Our Backs*, vol. 30, August 2000, pp. 12–15. Copyright © 2000 by Off Our Backs, Inc. Reproduced by permission.

vides an environment in which acts of rape are fostered. Look through any supposed women's publication and notice the ads that display women at the mercy of a man or at the mercy of the male gaze. Notice the articles that emphasize dependence and passivity and avoid portraying independence and strength in women. Watch TV shows that display precocious models of sexually manipulated teen-aged women. Walk into any bar and watch the women primp and the men pounce, and watch, too, as the number of unreported rapes turns into the number of women socialized into accepting this sort of sexual behavior as standard—not even recognizing rape when it occurs. Rape is part of the natural flora of our society and our world. . . .

A study of the rape culture done by the University of California at Davis found: "the high incidence of rape in this country is a result of the power imbalance between men and women. Women are expected to assume a subordinate relationship to men. Consequently rape can be seen as a logical extension of the typical interactions between men and women.". . .

Women are brainwashed into thinking that we HAVE to do certain things to be accepted [by men]. . . . This is the rape culture.

My back tenses, my voice gets higher and lighter. I smile excessively, all the while feeling ridiculous. There is a boy in the room. A boy with no particularly alluring energy, but every woman in the room is riveted. We all want him. Something has entered my consciousness and those are social germs of gender construction. If I stop to think about it (which women rarely do) I don't want him at all, but years of social training push a button in my spine that turns on Super Girl when there is a male presence. Super Girl is a combination of a bunch of different behaviors relegated to women. And this is what is engendered through the training program of prime-time romantic dramas and reinforced by real life interactions between men and women.

Unless we constantly struggle against social pressures, women are brainwashed into thinking that we HAVE to do certain things to be accepted. Women smile more than men, we take up less space, we defer to men as they interrupt our conversations, we apologize before stating an opinion, and we strive day in and day out to perfect our bodies for the male gaze. This is the rape culture. When men decide that they want, we give. When we say no, we apologize. Our no's are interrupted by their yes's. And we sexualize our bodies for the world of men and not for ourselves; therefore we don't love them enough to protect them. These small-seeming social actions translate into sexual assault as they reach the bedroom.

Young women and the rape culture

Because of feminism's many successes, women have been seduced into submission once again. In the beginning of the 21st century, many more women than not are convinced that we have reached equality with men. This is a dangerous conviction, primarily because it is not true. The reason the rape culture is endemic to American women is because we have the illusion that we exist in a safe space, where rape only happens to women who jog late at night in Central Park. The term "date rape" is often mocked among my peers as a creation by sexually insecure women. And feminism is a dirty word, as those of us with vocal feminist views know all too well.

Rape is endemic because it pervades every aspect of our complex social structure.

The advertisements and music videos depict women in skimpy clothing with beckoning looks on their faces. Women with small and impossible bodies are what we aspire to because that is what men are attracted to. And women are first and foremost supposed to be attractive to men. But women, particularly women in college, are also told that we are smart, liberated, equal to men, and have some inner goddess—strength. These contradictory messages can be confusing and keep us enthralled by the rape culture if we let the belief that we have social equality blind us to the subliminal messages embedded in the media.

To be a young woman today means to live with the rape culture in all its subtleties. It means to act in accordance with the roles that keep men forever in power. I may be a smart, educated, self-confident woman of the modern day, but any man who wants to can rape me because he is stronger. Not only physically stronger, but psychologically stronger because he was taught by the system to be aggressive and take what he feels he deserves. To be a young woman often means to buy *Glamour* and *Vogue* [women's magazines] and take the advice that pleases men. It means to fluctuate body weight to please the day's fashion archetype. Being a young woman today means to be unhappy if men don't like the way you look. I have cried many a night because of my big shoulders and my skinny, white legs, and I still struggle to find my own definition of what is sexy.

Cultural cures for rape

The media do not recognize rape as a cultural disease. When magazines or news programs do examine the subject, it is often under the guise of stranger rape or rape in severely abusive relationships. Or it is identified as a potentially passing epidemic or the actions of some psychopathic man. And the solution suggested by this same media is avoidance. Avoid dark streets (obviously), avoid bad situations (well, to most of us, a bar in general is a bad situation), avoid going out alone, walking alone, drinking too much, dressing too revealingly, being too aggressive, smiling too profusely, or acting too insecure. Basically the solution is to walk on tiptoes around men, and to take back the night by staying inside and watching a good movie. The solution to rape as it stands now is to let men continue to do this until women are too scared to leave their homes alone or in groups, or even to live alone because men hold the ultimate power of decision. Men hold in their big hands the power over women's sexual safety. That is simply not good enough.

Rape is endemic because it pervades every aspect of our complex social structure. In order to vaccinate against it, we would have to change many parts of society that people are fully comfortable with and accepting of. Patriarchy is still very much at work, only more subtly. There is a defiance of admitting weakness because weakness is devalued and to be raped in these fucked up days, is to be weak. Postmodern theory waxes on about inclusion and identity politics; liberals pretend equality has been achieved. And because of the code of sex-positive cool, young women accept these stances at face value and ignore the ongoing perpetuation of rape culture.

Rape is not an epidemic that spiked mysteriously in the mid-seventies when feminists called attention to it. It is not a sudden outbreak that can be cured with a single vaccine. It is an endemic social disease that pervades every walk of life imaginable. This is the rape culture—millions of small-seeming social germs translate into sexual assault as they reach the bedroom.

[Popular movies] depict rape as rough, unwanted sex, that is nevertheless sexy.

In rape-crisis training, I learned what makes men rape. And it is not some inbred sexual urge that is just part of man's biology. It is power and privilege. I learned what keeps women silent. It is fear. My experience with the rape culture wasn't the same as women who had the misfortune to be physically forced to have sex. But mine is frightening because I, like a zombie, played the cards I had been dealt and didn't even think about how seduced I was by the mainstream suggestions for male/female behaviors.

In my biology class I learned that smallpox has been virtually eradicated and only exists in isolated labs. It used to be a rampant epidemic. If science can stamp out such a pervasive disease, and if a developing economy can get rid of typhoid, then an aware and educated society with new values can eliminate the social germs of rape. We can stop rape in this new century—if we are ready to identify the aspects of our cultural environment that foster rape and eliminate them.

Rape culture: media and message

Something was taken from me the other day as I, in a fit of self-destruction, picked up *Glamour* magazine and decided to read it for pleasure. What was taken from me was my ironclad sense of immunity, because the advertisements and the articles got to me and made me hate myself and want to buy a cure over the counter. I do not feel safe when I look into the pages of pop culture and I feel even less safe when I watch TV.

Marx said one thing that nearly everyone knows: Religion is the Opiate of the Masses. And I am going to rephrase that and say that opiating the masses is the religion of media. People still have Jesus and Judaism, Mohammed and Hinduism as guides for moral conduct, but media has the youth culture in its grasp and a new kind of conduct is iterated as gospel. The media gives us gender roles and social norms to mimic and worship as creed. To disobey is to be outcast from the religion of normal, of popular.

Nearly every advertisement is sexist in some way. *Ms. Magazine* and *Bitch* have monthly critiques of ads that display the American way of misogyny through objectification of and disrespect to the female figure and to female existence. I have sent dozens in and never had one printed because the magazines simply receive too goddamn many each month. I started creating a notebook of clippings for myself, in case anyone ever needs validation of my radical feminist beliefs, needs my reason for fighting this particular battle. And it is full. After only a few months, it is full.

Capitalism is allowed to replicate the rape culture by selling it maniacally as sex.

So back to my day of self-destruction and *Glamour*. The cover was harmless enough, an unhealthy looking and slenderized Minnie Driver [film actress], a few quotes about how to have better sex and how men did not want model bodies (au contrarie, I found out inside the demonic covers). But, I told myself, I am confident. I am armed with feminist intent. I understand and hate the patriarchal system. I love myself the way I am. But unfortunately I did not believe me after seeing autumn's new fashions draped over unattainable, delicately beautiful frames. I failed to come through for me when I read a line that said *wear the red sequined dress that makes him pant and her narrow her eyes in envy*. And then I turned to this particular Candies [perfume] ad. And I stared, trying to convince myself that I was simply, too caught up in my "everyone hates women" thing and that I was being really humorless. But I couldn't do it this time. This time the media sexism, the rape culture, the patriarchy was too fucking blatant. They threw it in my face and dared me to freak out. I accept that dare. . . .

[In the Candies ad,] there is indeed a rock and roll dude pressing a key on the computer with a leering, self-satisfied smirk. And than button is, yes, causing a rocket to blast off directly up between the legs of a splayed out woman perched on top of the computer screen, who is coyly cheeking a bottle of something or other. What is the message? At the push of a button, a man can release a burning hot, compact phallus between a dumbly willing, hot as shit female. And she will just sit there and take it, love it, all the while just coveting her bottle of fragrance. This ad, apparently, sells perfume.

I am ready to never wear the stuff again. I am ready to just tear into Candies and tell someone off. I wrote some letters, made some calls—to no avail. I am just a humorless feminazi, apparently.

Unfortunately this style of ad is not rare. Candies has a whole campaign of misogynist, subtly violent ads that sell various products. You can hop onto their website and see a wide variety of images of violence against women in the name of "sex sells." They call it racy and they call it daring. I call it the rape culture. I call their game.

This ad is violent. Because it uses the idea of a rocket blasting off into a woman as a play on sex. It makes a woman victim to a smirking man and markets this as sexy. The world, or at least the majority of it, is convinced that this is sex. That we live in an era where violent sex is okay.

Portraying violence as sexy and acceptable

It is not just this ad that perpetuates the stereotypes and dangerous social constructions of gender in America. In the book *Cunt* (a book you should all read right now!), Inga Muscia encourages women to walk out of movies that have rape scenes. At first I wondered why. I thought that movie rape scenes must really show men how horrible rape is and encourage them not to do it. But then I thought about all the movies I have seen with rape scenes. Like *The Accused*, or *Kids*, or *American Psycho*. And I realized that these cinematic forays into the crime of rape make it sexy. They depict rape as rough, unwanted sex, that is nevertheless sexy. They show the frail, beautiful woman and the big, beautiful man engaged in sexual intercourse that just happens to be accompanied by mutters of no and some tears, or some serious drunken sleeping. Rape scenes in movies are geared to turn people on, not shock them. And as long as the public is being seduced by the myth that rape is about sex and not about power, and that rape is about lust and not oppressive violence, then the rape culture can continue to thrive and to destroy women.

Ads such as the Candies ad and the rape scenes in movies portray violence as sexy and acceptable. They seduce viewers into being believers in rape culture and help create another generation of rapists who believe that rape is not violence, but merely sexual intercourse that sometimes goes "wrong."

The only "good" rape scene I have ever seen is *Boys Don't Cry*, a movie about the true story of a transgender female to male who was discovered to be a woman born and was therefore raped brutally and violently. The movie showed that the men raping Brandon Teena were not doing it to get off sexually, but to violently enforce gender roles. They raped her because she had a vagina and she had threatened their concept of gender.

I can't really say I want to see more movies portray scenes like this either, because I threw up afterwards. I don't want to live in a place where we have to endure such realities. But I also don't want to live in a place that candy coats these realities into normative sexuality in order to support social roles and a culture that normalizes rape.

With a little chemical flowing through my blood I can convince myself to kiss and fondle like a good girl.

While ads and movies are normalizing rape, TV is busy making it just disappear entirely. When I was in high school there was an episode of the ever-popular *Beverly Hills 90210* that depicted a woman being coerced into sex by a regular on the show. A regular that everybody in the 90210 communities loved and respected did not stop having sex when he was asked to and then proceeded to convince the woman it was okay. He never intended to talk to her again, and when she called it rape, no one believed her. So far, so good. Pretty real, pretty accurate. But the end is bullshit as she forgives dear Steve and Steve's female friends relent and hug him and the next few episodes show him up to his old tricks and we never hear from the woman again. In that show the "incident" was not even labeled as rape. The mass media managed to wrap centuries of oppression into one tiny hour and depict it totally according to rape culture's social roles. The woman was portrayed as annoying, drunk, overly emotional, and clearly full of shame at having slept with Steve. Steve was portrayed as confident and popular, incredulous of her accusation, and unaware of his behavior.

By the time this particular episode appeared, I was over my 90210 worship. But man, in the old days I was devout. I wanted to live that life and would have mirrored nearly everything on that show in my own social life. And I imagine that many young women and men felt the same. That episode along with many other prime time dramas sent the incorrect message that rape is an oops on the boy's part and can be easily wrapped up and erased between commercials for toothpaste. But rape, sexual harassment, sexual assault, and coercion are in real life incredibly difficult emotional ordeals for women.

In this TV show, which represents a microcosm of the youth mainstream and their social assumptions, the gender norms that create the rape culture were reinforced and the reality of rape was pushed far into the subconscious of youthful viewers.

The power of TV and other media to influence the values, personalities, and lifestyles of all of us cannot be overestimated. With working parents' busy lives, children are often plopped in front of the cheapest babysitter to be found, TV. In a culture obsessed with sound bites and quick gratification, young women read blurbs in exploitive magazines and get advice from advertisements. In a culture seduced by the almighty dollar; capitalism is allowed to replicate the rape culture by selling it maniacally as sex. When I read that *Glamour* magazine I lost something. I lost the bet with myself that I, as a feminist, as a media-avoiding, enlightened rape counselor, would be able to manage to hold ground under the persuasion of God-like media images. If I lost, what about the masses of women who don't have an education in the field perceptions and social interactions? Today women learn to be women and men learn to be men immersed in rape culture; and the day ends and begins on the same note of silence from viewers of the mass media.

Rape culture: a personal story

I've met myself as a vulnerable woman, a woman who did not have the world by the balls with her intense feminist rhetoric, a woman who had failed to beat the invasive rape culture too many times.

I have many bad men in my life, some random, some more serious. Some that forever changed me into the scared, insecure person I am sometimes. But I am one who avoids such personal revelation, instead choosing to offer my knowledge and compassion to others while suffering silently inside.

I was trained for 40 plus hours to be a peer rape counselor, and my friend and trainer Melanie remembers my face during the sessions as one of boredom. She thought I was zonked out of my mind from being assaulted with constant information and having to sit through it for 8 or more hours a day. I suppose I have my facial muscles as trained as my thoughts to avoid giving anything away, because I was not bored. While Melanie looked at me and thought I was bored, this is what I was thinking:

In high school, I was not a popular girl. First came braces. Then came acne. Then came unpopular views, so by senior year I had not had huge amounts of experience in the socio-sexual sector. I am socially trained to be a heterosexual female, incomplete without the love or lust of a man. This incomplete feeling, this contrived loneliness that keeps me from loving myself instead, loving friends instead, shapes me into a woman dressing for the man. I wear better clothes and become some sort of flirt, constantly on in the presence of men, making jokes and meeting eyes, and I become attractive pretty quickly. College is a big sex fest. Put a few thousand men and women into an unpatrolled area with no parental authority and you are going to have sex. And I go to college in the era postsexual revolution, which means that I as a liberated young girl am supposed to be sex positive, into fucking many men and liking it. I begin my career as a pot head/drunk around this time as do many college coeds. Why do so many of us get wasted as a favorite weekend pastime? Maybe because we are giving ourselves the courage to play the roles that we have been rehearsing for years. Maybe because with a little chemical flowing through my blood I can convince myself to kiss and fondle like a good girl. I can convince myself that I want this like all of the boys say I do. I never call any of this sexual violence, oppression, or rape and it is so far in the past that I don't want to think about this now. I want it to stay the memory I created.

I have writhed beneath bodies with every muscle screaming no while my trained vocal chords made the appropriate sighs.

There was a boy who came to visit my first college often, he was a friend of a boy that I really liked and had hooked up with a few times. Nick, the boy I liked, did not return the feelings and I was resentful. His friend liked everything with a vagina and I was vulnerable enough to think I was more. We drank beers and talked about [the rock band] Pearl Jam, a love we both shared. We drunkenly went to my room, kicked my roommate out and went for it. I had never, ever been in a situation so aggressive in my life. The other boys of that year were soft in their sexual advances. He was writhing on top of me touching body parts that I never wanted him to touch, I wanted to make out and rub backs or something. I whispered slow down or whoa or something to no response other than moans and it'll be fine. I thought perhaps that the other boys hadn't really liked me and that TJ did and that this was how it was supposed to be. Rough, aggressive, with me powerless, with me on the bottom. A few red lights flashed at first but I was so scared to say no because why? Why? Because I want him to like me and I want Nick to be jealous and I want to be popular and sexy and not disappoint this boy on top of me by not allowing him to complete this charade. I want to be the cool chick who could fuck without feeling way more than I want to be the strong woman who took a stand and said get the hell out you are scaring me.

I remember feeling very small. I remember his whole body pressing down on me and not being able to kiss him back because I could not breathe. I remember not saying no. I remember wanting to. And thankfully, I remember Sara knocking on the door repeatedly looking for me because she knew where I was and who I was with and wanted to rescue me from certain sexual shame. I answered her calls so she knew I was in there, even though TJ said shhhhhh. She heard me and did not relent so I found my way up and he left and I never saw him again, but I never told anyone how uncomfortable I had been in that small dark room and how scary it was not to be able to breathe and how much I hated myself for disappointing him and not following through like a little prude. All I ever told anyone was that we had "hooked up." In my head at the time that was truth, I saw nothing integrally wrong with how it went down and I ignored my fear and my instinct and my red lights. It became legend and I was a girl who hooked up and I had lots of lovers.

Rejecting dating violence

If you read my diaries, you will not find a record of this event. You will find a record of declining happiness, an incline in drug use, and an eventual academic suspension from the university. You will never find me saying in those detailed pages that I was scared of boys and confused about sex roles because I did not think that I was. I did not realize that every boy that I met inspired fear in me, so I kept myself safe by having either unattainable crushes or hooking up with boys I knew I could control. I was Ali, the girl with the big mouth, who cut through the bullshit and said what she thought and who was sexy and smart and independent and a feminist, no less. I was protected. I was above physical sexual oppression. What had gone down in that little room was nothing more than me being inexperienced, than me letting him down, than me catching my breath and never thinking about it as such again. And this situation is not an isolated incident in my early sexual past. I have slept with men I didn't love and didn't even know because I didn't think I had the social standing to say no. I have writhed beneath bodies with every muscle screaming no while my trained vocal chords made the appropriate sighs. And I hated myself every second during and too many more afterwards.

I, too, am a victim of social construction. I, too, have the intense female desire to be liked; to fit into the dating paradigms configured by gendered social norms.

It took my intense week of counselor training to infiltrate the secure stone wall of created consciousness that had prevented me from recognizing my own penetrability. As a woman born, I am vulnerable not only to the physical penetration of rape, but the mental penetration of the rape culture that socializes my womanhood. I didn't say no when I felt uncomfortable, I felt bad for disappointing him, I was rescued from SHAME not danger, and I convinced myself that the aggressive sexual attention is HOOKING up and not some fucked up manifestation of TJ's male privilege and power over my unsuspecting and passive female constitution.

I am lucky to have friends lurking around corners, but it is not always set up as such. Situations like this are normal, endemic to the dating scene. And nobody seems to recognize the violence proffered by magazine ads and television shows, by MTV videos or cigarette billboards. [Folksinger and feminist] Ani Difranco said "We learn America like a script," and I agree. Men and women are planted into roles and their character studies are media images.

I met myself as a vulnerable woman who performed programmed dialogue. It is now my job to make her stronger and write her new lines with the conviction and self-confidence that women deserve.

8

Acquaintance Rape by Athletes Is a Widespread Problem

Jeffrey R. Benedict

Jeffrey R. Benedict is a sociologist who has conducted extensive research on the problem of college athletes and violence against women. He is the author of Athletes and Acquaintance Rape, *from which the following viewpoint is excerpted.*

Professional and college athletes have become renowned for their sexual promiscuity and are viewed by the public as having easy access to sex with female "groupies." This commonly held perception has insulated athletes from legal consequences when women accuse them of acquaintance rape. Jurors are not easily convinced that high-profile athletes would need to resort to force in order to have sex with women who are stereotyped as eager groupies. As a result, prosecutors are frequently persuaded to lessen or drop rape charges against athletes, even though acquaintance rape by athletes is a widespread problem. Both the sports industry and the American public need to send a stronger message to athletes that sexually assaulting women will no longer be tolerated.

In August 1995, prosecutors in La Crosse, Wisconsin, received a complaint alleging that numerous members of the New Orleans Saints football team sexually assaulted a woman in Sanford Hall on the University of Wisconsin campus where the team was being housed during its preseason summer camp. After a police officer in a patrol car spotted a woman crying outside the dormitory at a predawn hour, he approached her and asked if she was in need of help. The victim told the officer that she had been raped and held against her will by a number of Saints football players after having voluntarily accompanied a player to his room earlier that evening. A witness who had been outside the dorm moments before the victim emerged confirmed to the officer that she heard screams coming from the floor on which the Saints were staying.

Unwilling to convict athletes

The victim was shuttled to a nearby hospital for examination. Meanwhile, police investigators were dispatched to the dorm. They began by interviewing the two players staying in the room where the alleged incident took place. Once inside, the officers saw a pair of women's panties on the floor (the victim left her panties behind in her attempt to escape the room). Before police seized the panties as evidence, one of the players in the room began rummaging around in the area where the panties were located. He then asked permission to use the bathroom, and police discovered the panties were suddenly missing. The player was searched and the panties were discovered stuffed in his pants.

With the district attorney's office soon joining the investigation, a total of 30 players were interviewed. The players named by the accuser did not deny sexual contact. The following excerpt is from the prosecutor's report:

> Player 1 . . . and Player 2 did lie down and took their clothes off. . . . He [Player 1] stated that he and Player 2 did perform sexual intercourse with her and that she also had oral sex with him. He stated that at one point when she was having oral sex with Player 2 that he had sexual intercourse with her from behind. . . . When Player 9 entered the room . . . he took his clothes off and then attempted to put a condom on. . . . Player 1 stated that he specifically remembers seeing Player 5 standing in the doorway because he made the comment that he couldn't even get into the room with all the guys in there. ("Investigation Summary," 1995)

Nonetheless, after completing his investigation, prosecutor Ron Kind declined to press charges. "I believe that the credibility of the woman who reported the assaults would be insufficient to convince a jury beyond a reasonable doubt that the sexual contact she had with numerous players was not consensual," said Kind ("Declination Report," 1995). The decision appears callous and unjust in light of the players' conduct. Yet, Kind's decision is consistent with the growing trend among prosecutors to dismiss sexual assault charges against professional and college athletes for lack of evidence. Out of 217 felony complaints of sexual assault against athletes filed between 1986 and 1995, 100 were dismissed by law enforcement, primarily due to insufficient proof to surmount the hurdle of reasonable doubt. Of the remaining 117 that resulted in an indictment, 51 resulted in dropped charges or were pleaded down to misdemeanors.

High esteem, eroded restraint

Dimissals and watered-down convictions are frequently met with harsh criticism by the media, women's groups, and victims' advocates. But the criticism has been inappropriately directed at law enforcement. It is the public that dictates whether athletes will be held accountable in these cases. Law enforcement's skittish approach to trying athletes for alleged acquaintance rape is predicated on jurors' unwillingness to convict athletes. Of the 66 athletes who were brought to trial on charges of rape during this time frame, only 6 were convicted. Moreover, these 66 cases represented the cases with the strongest likelihood of a conviction (evidence of physical injury, timely reporting, strong victim, and in some cases multiple defendants—which would seem to refute the consent element). Thus, the inability to gain convictions even in these cases offers a clear illustration of the high esteem in which jurors hold athletes and the corresponding distrust of women who accuse athletes of abuse.

Jurors hold athletes [in high esteem] and . . . distrust . . . women who accuse athletes of abuse.

As in most acquaintance rape cases, conviction turns on the credibility of the accuser and the accused. When an athlete is the defendant, jurors are routinely faced with the question: Why would a famous athlete resort to force when he can have any woman he wants? Although both sexist and arrogant, this is the most natural defense for a powerful male celebrity to raise. This approach is often clever enough to fool jurors. Yet athletes' arrogant claims of having women readily available for their sexual desires raises a more relevant question: When celebrated athletes become so accustomed to having their sexual urges fulfilled on demand, are they capable of restraining themselves when confronted by a woman who says "no"?

With their power of self-restraint eroded by excessive sexual indulgence, many athletes become unwilling to accept rejection by women. Moreover, having never been held accountable by coaches, fans, the public, or the courts for ignoring a woman's wishes, there is little incentive for athletes to respect the word "no" from a woman. . . .

Sexual license

The lion's share of rape complaints against athletes comes from victims who are socially acquainted with their perpetrator. Under these circumstances, as is the case in any complaint of acquaintance rape, proof beyond a reasonable doubt is difficult to establish. There are seldom any witnesses; physical evidence is usually sparse; and the cases are reduced to a he-said-she-said contest. But there are additional obstacles to a successful prosecution when the alleged perpetrator is a renowned athlete.

Ironically, athletes' increasingly deviant sexual habits are one of the most influential factors in insulating them from legal consequences when women accuse them of rape. Sexual indulgence has become a trademark of modern-day popular athletes. An increasing number of athletes publicly boast of rampant sexual promiscuity by themselves and their teammates. The public's exposure to athletes' sexual practices has popularized the term "groupie," a label loosely applied to women who hang around athletes and often engage in sex with them.

Clearly, there are women who pursue athletes for sexual purposes. But groupie behavior (the pursuit of sexual relationships with famous athletes) is peculiar to an extremely small segment of women. Nonetheless, these women are a prevalent fixture in the social life of professional athletes. Moreover, their complicity reinforces the athletes' attitude of sexual license. In short, the jock-groupie tango is the engine driving the socialization process undergone by many athletes, which churns out an image of women as sexually compliant. The sex-for-fame commerce that exists between athletes and groupies undermines autonomy and trivializes the fundamental component of consent. Ultimately, athletes' indulgence in such relationships reduces their ability to distinguish between force and consent.

Whereas women who exhibit groupie behavior are certainly susceptible to victimization, an even greater threat exists for women who, despite having no explicit sexual interest in an athlete, come into social contact with a player and naively traverse consensual boundaries. Regardless of the circumstances, defense attorneys capitalize on the public's perception of groupies and generally categorize any woman who accuses an athlete of sexual misconduct as a groupie. Depicting the accuser as either a vengeful or fame-seeking groupie who has targeted a famous athlete invokes, at very least, the premise of implied consent. Defense lawyers seldom mention it, but the frequent sexual misconduct charges levied against athletes arise from a deviant lifestyle lived by some athletes that combines the lethal combination of being free from social responsibility and having unlimited access to random, consensual sexual encounters.

Defense attorneys . . . categorize any woman who accuses an athlete of sexual misconduct as a groupie.

When an alleged incident of sexual violence occurs under these circumstances, neither a victim's claim of rape nor a professional athlete's plea of innocence is easily established. The obscurity of consent gives defense attorneys the upper hand, as their only task is to establish doubt in the minds of jurors. Prosecutors, on the other hand, must prove the use of force beyond a reasonable doubt.

Research on victim-rapist relationships reveals that rape is typically not an act of random violence, but rather exploitation of women who felt comfortable enough to be alone with their attacker. Attorney Susan Estrich, who popularized the term "simple rape," concluded that most rapes involving acquaintances are without signs of physical struggle, weapon use, or eyewitnesses. According to Estrich, the absence of corroborating evidence is used by defense lawyers as an indication that consensual sex occurred, as opposed to real rape. Both court officials and jurors are receptive to rape myths because of pervasive stereotypes about female sexuality. Perhaps nowhere is sexual stereotyping more distorted than between athletes and women.

The influence of rape myths is a powerful diversionary tool. By injecting doubt, myths obscure the distinction between where voluntary action ends and coercion begins. Former New York City sex crimes prosecutor Alice Vachss pointed out that only two defenses are available to a defendant accused of acquaintance rape: "It never happened" and "consent." Athletes almost exclusively choose the latter.

Expecting sex, acting with impunity

The concept of consent is premised on physical power to act and free use of that power. But celebrated athletes have an unsurpassed combination of power and popularity, often placing the women who are with them on unequal ground from the outset. Former Los Angeles Laker Earvin "Magic" Johnson insisted that it is not unusual for women to offer their bodies for the pure sexual exploitation of professional athletes. As a result, some sports stars reach a point where they come to expect sex from all females who vie for their attention.

The expectation of sex that some athletes come to acquire is consistent with research suggesting that "rape-supportive attitudes are socially acquired beliefs" [by Mary Koss]. In 1988, Mary Koss conducted a survey of 2,972 men and found that "[m]ost men (88%) who reported an assault that met the legal definition of rape were adamant that their behavior was definitely not rape." According to [researcher] Gregory Matoesian, this does not mean that all rapists are lying, "but rather that they may actually be more likely . . . to interpret sexual interactions as consensual, even if they involve various levels of physical force and coercion."

Much of the casual sex engaged in by athletes is seldom the result of affirmatively expressed consent or vocally conveyed resistance. Rather, there is a condition of sexual drift, or an instinctive flow toward sex, that is encouraged by the elevation of male athletes to cultural icons. Although much of the indiscriminate sexual activity participated in by professional athletes is the result of consent—thereby legally permissible—this atmosphere is nonetheless conducive to opportunities for felony rape.

Repeated sexual encounters with numerous partners narrows an athlete's view of women and convinces players that they can act with impunity toward any woman who vies for their attention. Mary Koss found that "the greater number of sexual partners a man has had, the greater the likelihood that he will have been sexually assaultive at least once." In this context, a player may either engage in an act or acts that go beyond an acquaintance's will, or mistake a woman's behavior for what he views to be consistent with groupie behavior. Ensuing sexual advances clearly complicate matters.

Repeated sexual encounters with numerous partners . . . convinces players that they can act with impunity toward any woman.

The nature of these relationships and the subsequent circumstances surrounding a complainant's claim of being criminally violated present law enforcement officials with inherent obstacles that deter the likelihood of successful criminal prosecution. Rape statutes in most states define rape as "the unlawful carnal knowledge of a woman by a man forcibly and against her will." The courts consider a man's disregard for a woman's resistance to intercourse as a brutally violent act of commission, second only to murder in seriousness. Incidents of acquaintance and date rape, by definition, involve victims who knew their attacker and voluntarily agreed to be alone with him. Although such circumstances often provide a context for arguments of implied consent, rape laws make no allowance for men who presume privacy is a license for sex. Furthermore, most state statutes, including Indiana, Massachusetts, and Washington, . . . stipulate that a woman maintains her autonomy to refuse intercourse even after she has engaged in other consensual acts of sex.

Whereas a woman's right to consent exists legally and socially in theory, it is often difficult to determine in practice where consent stops and force begins in situations involving two or more participants who have had previous sexual relations. As a general rule, accused athletes take special advantage of this circumstance and admit sexual contact while denouncing any implication of force. Defense attorneys buttress these claims by routinely denouncing almost all accusers as groupies.

Victims face skepticism

When an athlete is identified as the perpetrator of a sex crime, prosecutors are typically confronted with an accuser who willfully accompanied the defendant to his bedroom, participated in some form of consensual activity—frequently sexual in nature—with the defendant immediately prior to the episode she describes as a rape, and may have even had associations with other professional athletes. Women who willfully enter into promiscuous encounters with star athletes compromise their autonomy once they enter a player's bedroom, whether it be a hotel or personal residence. In addition to the obvious fact that professional athletes are physically superior to most men—let alone women—professional players generally interpret a woman's willful entrance into their bedroom as a license to pursue their self-gratifying objectives with no concern for the acquaintance's desires.

The sports industry has demonstrated a clear callousness toward the abuse of women by players.

Although women regularly enter and exit these brief sexual encounters without complaint, they are nonetheless susceptible to tremendous skepticism should they in fact become the victim of an assault. Under these circumstances, their consensual behavior preceding an incident of sexual assault subjects them to serious questions concerning credibility. As a result, women who are criminally violated in the bedrooms of professional athletes provide defense attorneys with character evidence that is potentially very persuasive in creating "reasonable doubt" in a juror's mind.

Furthermore, the prosecution is aware that the defense lawyers who will be bringing these facts to the attention of a jury are the most skilled and renowned litigators that money can buy, because of the considerable resources that professional athletes can muster for their defense. The superior skill of defense counsel is critical to these cases, due to the fact that rape cases are frequently absent of eyewitnesses. This fact compels the jury to ascertain the truth based on the believability of two opposing accounts of the same incident. Under this scenario, defense attorneys emphasize attributes of the accuser that undermine her credibility. Lawyers who represent professional players have the peculiar advantage of citing the unique social life of celebrity athletics, where there is an abundance of opportunity for illicit sex, as a reasonable explanation for implied consent.

Despite the victimization of women who had no desire for sexual involvement with their athlete-perpetrators, the circumstances of the athletes' subculture furnishes defense attorneys with a context to depict all accusers as groupies. The existence of groupie behavior exposes all victims of abuse to being branded a groupie.

The prevalence of groupie behavior provides a significant strength to the defense of professional athletes even in cases where the accused has exhibited no groupie behavior. Although the likelihood of successful criminal prosecution of felony rape charges is considerably enhanced when the prosecution can demonstrate to the jury that the accuser is not a groupie, the defense is nonetheless bolstered in its attempt to create reasonable doubt by associating the accuser with groupies.

A final, but no less important, issue complicating the prosecution of athletes for sex crimes is the race factor. There is often a racial overtone to many of these cases because of the high likelihood that an alleged athlete perpetrator will be black. For example, as of 1996, over 80% of the players in the NBA and nearly 70% of NFL players were black. Due to overrepresentation of blacks in professional sports, there is a corresponding overrepresentation of black athletes among the athlete-perpetrators. The shortage of white players in the ranks of celebrity athletics explains in large part, the discrepancy between the number of white and black athletes being arrested for violating women. As further evidence of this point, Canada is seeing a growing number of its celebrity athletes being charged with violating women. A key distinction is that nearly all of the alleged perpetrator athletes in Canada are white males, a fact easily explained by virtue of hockey being the culture's top sport.

Despite the fact that race has no causal connection to men's abuse of women, defense lawyers and other supporters of the athletes will not resist raising racism as a motive for prosecuting players. Although there is rarely any basis to such accusations, the threat of being labeled racist serves to put law enforcement and others on notice to proceed with extra caution when investigating these matters.

These circumstances impede prosecutors when considering whether or not to present a case before a jury. As a result, district attorneys are frequently discouraged from seeking an indictment, or they are otherwise persuaded to entertain plea bargains more readily. It is rare for prosecutors to win a successful trial verdict in rape cases against professional athletes, due to the ease with which defense lawyers can portray victims as groupies. Jurors have proved to be too enamored, too trusting, and too forgiving of celebrated athletes who violate women. . . .

Solutions

The roots to sexual violence run deep and are not found in the mere participation in organized athletics. Violence against women is pervasive throughout society and is far too complex a problem for the entertainment industry to solve. But the deviant social lifestyles embraced by so many of today's high-profile athletes increases the frequency of reported incidents of sexual assault in the ranks of ballplayers. Although the sports industry cannot be expected to shoulder the task of completely eradicating the problem of athletes' violence against women, there are measures that can be taken to stem the increasing number of assaults.

Nonetheless, the sports industry has demonstrated a clear callousness toward the abuse of women by players. Repeatedly denying the presence of any particular problem among athletes, league representatives and coaches have proved to be altogether unwilling and incapable of taking any initiative to curb the problem. Moreover, the plentiful resources of teams, league front offices, and players unions are more often used to support abusive players. Thus, it is incumbent on others—colleges who recruit athletes, law enforcement, and the public—to act affirmatively to combat the frequent abuse of women by high-profile athletes.

Colleges

There needs to be a much stronger message of intolerance sent when male athletes first abuse women—long before they arrive in the professional ranks and earn millions of dollars. Many of the professional athletes who are arrested for violating women have a history of prior mistreatment of women, often reaching all the way back to high school.

Due to the unique relationship between scholarship athletes and institutions of higher learning, universities and colleges are in a position to take steps to prevent recurring abuse of women by athletes. When a college athlete is arrested or otherwise formally charged with sexually assaulting a woman, schools should immediately suspend the accused player's scholarship. This should be done prior to the school independently determining the merits of the complaint. Following the scholarship suspension, school officials can assess whether the facts warrant revoking the scholarship altogether pending the outcome of criminal proceedings.

Ultimately, it is the public . . . who have the most influential power to curb athletes' violence against women.

Short of concluding—prior to the disposition of the criminal case—that the alleged sexual assault indeed occurred, school officials have sufficient grounds to revoke a scholarship if either of the following circumstances exist: (a) additional student code-of-conduct violations that do not constitute criminal conduct, but are nonetheless associated with the more serious pending sexual assault allegations; or (b) a previous record, albeit unrelated to the case at hand, of criminal misbehavior by the athlete that has led to arrest, indictment, or conviction.

An illustration is provided in a sexual assault complaint filed against five Brigham Young University (BYU) football players in 1995. After the five players were reported to the Provo, Utah, police, both civil and university officials conducted investigations. The incident involved, among other things, alcohol consumption—a violation of the school's code of conduct. With the players admitting to participating in consensual sex with the complainant, but denying the use of force, law-enforcement authorities declined to file formal charges on the basis of insufficient evidence. Nonetheless, BYU officials expelled all five athletes, despite never determining the validity of the rape allegation. Once the school's internal investigation found that the incident entailed violations of other aspects of the school's policies, the athletic department was notified that the players were no longer eligible to be on scholarship.

Law enforcement and the public

Although criminal complaints against recognizable athletes represent a statistically insignificant number of the overall sexual assault complaints filed with police and prosecutors, these few cases draw the most public attention. Violence against women perpetrated by athletes tends to be a touchstone of society's larger problem with the mistreatment of women. For example, there was little public discourse about domestic violence prior to the O.J. Simpson case. This is not to say that cases against athletes deserve more attention from law enforcement. But those in position to make determinations on whether to charge an accused player should be less skeptical of complainants' accounts and more willing to subject accused athletes to vigorous investigation.

Although the law enforcement community is becoming increasingly aware of the less than exemplary attitudes and actions of star athletes, there remains a reluctance on the part of investigators to arrest players accused of sexual assault by women who appear to have initiated the relationship. Moreover, prosecutors are even more hesitant to indict on the basis of a complaint brought by an accuser who may appear to have sought out her perpetrator. Although the public's impatience with less than pure victims in acquaintance rape cases makes law enforcement's trepidation understandable on the one hand, investigators and prosecutors must nonetheless hold these male role models to the social standards contained in the law.

By failing to indict athletes accused of sexual assault, law enforcement is essentially throwing in the towel and adding to the perception of license held by many of these perpetrators. Perhaps even more damaging, the public—particularly the younger generation of sports fans—sees athletic ability being treated as an exemption pass from the demands of justice.

Ultimately, it is the public—the consumers who finance the salaries of high-priced athletes—who have the most influential power to curb athletes' violence against women. Money is the engine driving professional sports. In order to change behavior and attitudes, the millions of American spectators must give sports leagues an incentive to take action against abusive players. But Americans are complacent when it comes to watching criminal athletes as long as they perform adequately on the field. There is little moral resolve to resist paying to see and cheering for athletes who are abusive to women—or who commit other types of crimes. Rather, there is a collective washing of the hands, as if to concede that heroes are no longer pure and little can be done to change that.

Unfortunately, this approach is unacceptable due to the growing numbers of youth and younger children who look to male athletes as examples. Whether or not choosing an athlete as a role model is good judgment, kids have nonetheless elected them as their heroes. Thus, there must be more willingness on the part of teachers, parents, youth-league coaches, and other adults to resist patronizing criminally abusive athletes. The forgive-and-forget, boys-will-be-boys approach cannot be tolerated. Until the public demonstrates their disdain for high-profile males who violate women, incidents of sexual assault by athletes will only increase.

9

The Use of Date-Rape Drugs Is Increasing

Karen J. Gordon

Karen J. Gordon is a freelance writer concerned with issues affecting women. She is a member of Feminists for Life of America, an organization working to end violence against women that publishes the American Feminist, *a quarterly newsletter from which the following viewpoint was selected.*

Studies indicate that 15 percent of female college students have been the victims of rape, and date rape remains a serious problem on college campuses. A disturbing trend is the rise of rapists who secretly add sedatives and powerful synthetic drugs to their victims' drinks, rendering them defenseless against an assault. Women must remain on the lookout for drug rapists at social gatherings and bars and never accept drinks from strangers. The advent of rape drugs is putting more women at risk of rape—individuals and institutions must do more to eliminate the underlying attitudes behind this crime of power.

Rebecca (a pseudonym), a first-year college student, thought the young man was trustworthy. He was polite and observant of social graces. At the party, Rebecca remembers, "I was definitely being encouraged to drink." As she came out of the restroom into the hallway, he was there, all 6'4" of him, directing her into an adjoining room. She felt uncomfortable when he kissed her, but not scared. But then he got rough. "He forced me to have oral sex with him. He held my hair and intimidated me to where he didn't have to use a lot of physical force. I thought, 'Oh my God, if I don't do what this guy says, he's already shown that he's going to hurt me.' I was like a rag doll to him. He scooped me up and put me on the bed and then he was on top of me. He was so big, there was no way I was getting out from under him."

Although she didn't realize it at the time, Rebecca was a victim of acquaintance rape (also called "date rape"). She is not alone. According to a 1998 survey jointly funded by the Department of Health and Human Ser-

Karen J. Gordon, "Predators on Campus: The Rise in Rape Drugs," *American Feminist*, vol. 6, Fall 1999, pp. 7–9. Copyright © 1999 by Feminists for Life of America. Reproduced by permission.

vices and the Department of Justice, nearly 1 in 5 American women is a survivor of rape or attempted rape. The number of rapes on college campuses is comparable. A national survey undertaken in 1985 by Mary P. Koss (now a professor of psychology at the University of Arizona) indicated that 15% of female students on college campuses are survivors of rape and a further 11% are survivors of attempted rape. The Bureau of Justice Statistics reports that 77% of violent crimes against women, including rape and incest, are committed by someone women know. Acquaintance rape on college campuses is prevalent.

Women can attempt to protect themselves by 1) communicating clearly about what they do and do not want to do, 2) trusting their own instincts, and 3) understanding that alcohol and drugs are often related to rape. Unfortunately, caution does not always prevent attack. If a woman is raped, local sexual-assault service organizations can help. "We support the survivor in many ways. We help her work through the system, from going to the hospital to filing a police report, if that's what she chooses to do," says Elizabeth McCravy, community education coordinator at Sexual Assault Support Services in Eugene, Oregon.

Powerful synthetic drug[s] . . . are used by sexual predators to render their victims defenseless.

In predator cases in which the rapist first drugs his victim (often by slipping something into her drink), paying attention to the first warning signs is crucial. Flunitrazepam (Rohypnol), a sedative in the Valium family, and gamma hydroxybutyrate (GHB), a powerful synthetic drug recently promoted for body building, are used by sexual predators to render their victims defenseless. What is especially disturbing about these drugs is the memory loss that occurs, leaving the victim unable to remember what she did, or what was done to her. When mixed with alcohol, both Rohypnol and GHB can be fatal.

Rohypnol, illegal in the United States but legally prescribed worldwide, has many street names: roofies, roaches, LaRoche (for its manufacturer, Hoffman-La Roche, Inc.), ruffles, and R2. When crushed and slipped into a drink, it is colorless, odorless and tasteless. In the first 20 to 30 minutes after ingestion, drunken-like symptoms appear—confusion and impaired motor skills and speech. Within two hours, most victims lose consciousness. Said Los Angeles Police Department detective Trinka D. Porrata, in a statement before the U.S. House of Representatives Subcommittee on Oversight and Investigations, "It seems from my exposure that much of the worldwide use of flunitrazepam is abuse . . . . [T]he manufacturer doesn't want to give up this drug worldwide since it generates more than $100 million per year for them."

GHB is another extremely dangerous drug. Like Rohypnol, GHB is colorless and odorless when mixed in a drink, but it may leave a slightly salty or bitter taste. On the street it's called Liquid Ecstasy, Grievous Bodily Harm or Liquid-G. It is often used as an experience enhancer, and it can cause heightened sexual desire. "GHB is on the rise and is a lot more dangerous (than Rohypnol)," says Bob Nichols, assistant state's attorney and a leading drug-rape prosecutor with the Sex Crimes Unit in Fort Lauderdale, Florida. "It's even more of a nightmare. It takes a capful of GHB to incapacitate somebody, and you can mix up a gallon with ingredients from a local hardware store for about $10." The effects of GHB vary from person to person and can include dizziness, confusion, severe drowsiness, and loss of consciousness. Symptoms are noticeable in about 15 minutes. "It's kind of hard to say because GHB is always a different strength," says Nichols. "There are hundreds of recipes on the Internet, and you never know how strong it is." According to Porrata, "GHB is perhaps the youngest in terms of discovery by abusers, though it is now literally exploding around the world."

More women at risk

Among the many hot spots that Porrata lists for these rape drugs: 1) College/high school gatherings and 2) restaurants and clubs catering to 21–35-year-olds with college degrees. Because these drugs are widely used, drinks should never be shared or left unattended, and women should avoid drinking from punch bowls and other open containers. They should never accept drinks from men at bars when the drinks have not been ordered from a bartender. If a woman wakes up feeling fuzzy, experiences memory lapse, or cannot account for a period of time, she may have unknowingly ingested Rohypnol or GHB. In such a case, preservation of physical evidence is critical, and women are advised not to shower or change clothes. Traces of Rohypnol stay in the system in a detectable form for up to three days, but GHB is gone in 12 hours.

Drinks should never be shared or left unattended, and women should avoid drinking from punch bowls and other open containers.

Anyone who thinks she may have been dosed with these drugs should go to a hospital for drug-toxicity testing as soon as possible. It is a mistake, though, to think that a positive test is required for police to pursue the case. "There's a lot of undercover work that can be done," says Nichols. "No matter how poor their recollection is, or whether they took the drugs themselves, or whatever they think of their case, I encourage victims to call the police. Because even if the police can't do something about it, they can at least document that this particular person seems to have a history of it, or this particular bar had this occur in it. If nobody speaks up then nothing happens."

Brett A. Sokolow, a specialist in campus safety and director of Campus Outreach Services, says, "I don't like to call Rohypnol and GHB date rape drugs. I know everyone does, but the fact of the matter is that a lot of people who use Rohypnol to perpetrate crimes are not dates. They're not even acquaintances. I would refer to it as a drug that is used to rape. We emphasize if you've had two beers and you feel like you've just had 10, if at any point you feel a stronger reaction to a substance than you expect to have, immediately get to a hospital. Have somebody take you and get tested. It's not worth the risk of what might happen later on."

Sokolow writes in "To Hear, Or Not to Hear Rape, Is the Question?": "It is estimated that one rape occurs on every college campus in this country every 21 hours." What is being done to address this problem? Many campuses have 24-hour hotlines. Prevention, safety and peer education programs are flourishing. Concerned women and men on campuses throughout the country have established rape awareness programs. The Campus Security Act of 1990 requires colleges to promote awareness of rape and other sex offenses. At least 70 colleges nationwide have implemented sexual assault policies and procedures from the guidebook *Total Sexual Assault Risk Management Strategies for Colleges* by Sokolow and Katie Koestner, founder of Campus Outreach Services. The issue of college adjudication of rape/sexual assault cases is controversial. Some administrators feel a duty to the students, while others think that hearing rape cases requires trained adjudicators. If colleges choose not to hear these cases, however, the victims lose again because the backlog for criminal rape prosecution is up to two years.

Action is being taken against acquaintance rape on college campuses, but the problem persists. The advent of drugs like Rohypnol and GHB puts even more women at risk. And although rape is a sexual act, it is actually a crime of power. The rape of women will begin to decrease only when individuals and institutions take collective action to examine and eliminate the underlying attitudes and causes.

10

The Most Dangerous and Widely Used Drug— Alcohol—Is Still Available Everywhere

Kim Ode

Kim Ode is a staff writer at the Star Tribune, *a daily newspaper in Minneapolis, Minnesota, from which this viewpoint is taken.*

Efforts to ban the importation and sale of drugs used by rapists to attack unsuspecting women are an important step in the fight against date rape. Alcohol, however, remains the date rapist's drug of choice and is associated with the overwhelming majority of sexual assault cases. Young women must become more aware of how alcohol impairs decision-making ability—leaving them vulnerable to physical harm—and exercise greater caution when drinking in certain social situations.

In the war against date rape, the little triumphs count. But let's not get drunk on victory, for although one weapon has been damaged, a vast arsenal remains intact.

The U.S. Food and Drug Administration urged manufacturers this month [January 1999] to recall the nutritional supplement gamma butyrolactone, or GBL. The supplement, sold in Minnesota under the brand names Revivarant and RenewTrient, has legitimate medical uses in treating narcolepsy, a condition that causes people to have sudden attacks of deep sleep. But some users showed up in emergency rooms vomiting and disoriented or, at the worst, in comas. GBL claims to do a Franklin Planner's worth of other tasks: stave off depression, enhance memory and vision, aid weight loss, boost athletic ability, build muscles. It might even help thicken skin and restore thinning hair. But it also might induce sleep and serve as an aphrodisiac. In scumbag terms, it's a potential date rape drug.

When people ingest GBL, it breaks down into the drug known as

GHB, or gamma hydroxybutyrate, also known as "liquid ecstasy." Other nicknames? "Grievous Bodily Harm" and "Easy Lay." GBL and GHB are poor relations of the well-known date rape drug Rohypnol. The U.S. government banned importation of that drug, but it remains available. Late last year [1998], Rohypnol manufacturer Hoffmann-LaRoche reformulated the sedative so that it turns clear liquids blue and some dark liquids cloudy, thereby alerting unsuspecting people.

Alcohol is the drug associated with 70 to 90 percent of . . . sexual assault cases.

Dr. Andrew Topliff of the Minnesota Poison Control System was one of two doctors who alerted the Centers for Disease Control about adverse reactions to GBL. He's hopeful that creative legislation will be developed to deal with the potential for abuse and yet recognize GBL's useful medical qualities.

The date rape concern is absolutely legitimate, but GBL and GHB are small potatoes compared with the huge amount of a much more widely used date rape drug that remains on shelves everywhere: alcohol.

Date rape drug of choice

Topliff calls booze "the date rape drug of choice," a status it has held for hundreds of years. Although society tolerates and even encourages its consumption, alcohol is the drug associated with 70 to 90 percent of the sexual assault cases he has observed.

Statistics at the Hennepin County [Minnesota] Medical Center's Sexual Assault Resource Service tell the same tale.

The better someone knows the assailant, the less likely she is to report a rape, so date rape statistics are significantly underreported, according to director Linda Ledray. Of the 630 sexual assault victims she worked with last year, about 60 percent were raped by someone they knew—and almost half of those cases involved alcohol.

"Women are more vulnerable when they're drinking," Ledray said. "They make bad choices. They do all kinds of things they wouldn't ordinarily do. That doesn't make it their fault. It's still the man who is taking advantage of them."

Some teenage girls contend—as they have for decades—that alcohol lets them duck responsibility for having sex. In "Venus in Blue Jeans," psychologist Natalie Bartle cites a survey of 750 girls between the ages of 12 and 19; almost 90 percent cite drinking as a major factor leading to sex.

"Girls are forfeiting their own decision-making processes to the whims of alcohol," she wrote, "and in an odd twist, they feel that drinking allows them to retain some self-respect if they do have sex."

Topliff isn't a prohibitionist or a teetotaler. "I drink alcohol myself, but again, with moderation. The problem is that there's a certain segment of society that doesn't do things in moderation."

We have warnings that try to address that: In little labels on bottles of booze, the surgeon general warns about the dangers of alcohol, stating that drinking during pregnancy may lead to birth defects, that alcohol impairs one's ability to drive a car or operate machinery, and that it may cause health problems.

Wineries, breweries, and distilleries all urge us to enjoy their products in moderation, but the reasons cited are almost always about maintaining our ability to drive—to stay alive and to avoid killing others—and not about the other dangers of drinking until we're drunk.

Alcohol impairs us physically, but it also impairs our ability to make wise decisions, which in certain situations may make us vulnerable to physical harm. That's why friends shouldn't let friends date drunk.

11

Men Must Fight Date Rape

Brendan Loy

Brendan Loy is a student at the University of Southern California and a contributor to the student newspaper the Daily Trojan, *where this viewpoint appeared as a column.*

If more male college students came to realize that date rape leaves its victims with long-term emotional harm, the number of date rape incidents on college campuses would significantly decrease. Many college men, however, remain oblivious to the harm they cause; they participate in a date rape culture in which it is acceptable to ply women with alcohol and engage in nonconsensual sex. Men must join the fight against date rape by speaking out against sexual assault and treating women with human decency and respect.

Women often proclaim, much to the chagrin of their male friends, that "all men are pigs." This, of course, is not true.

Too many jerks

But there are far too many pigs—pigs, and sexual criminals—among us. Events such as Tuesday night's "Take Back the Night" rally, an annual candlelight vigil that concludes with a heart-wrenching "speak out" in which survivors of sexual assault share their tragic stories, make that fact painfully clear. I wish every man in America, or at least every male student at University of Southern California (USC), could attend Take Back the Night and listen to these women's stories. Then they would know what every survivor and every friend of a survivor knows: One night of reckless "fun" for an unthinking jerk can create a lifetime of pain, anguish and fear for that jerk's sex object of choice, who also happens to be a living, breathing human being.

I am convinced that if every man saw what I've seen—the long-term impact that date rape has on its victims—the number of incidents on college campuses would plummet. Perhaps this is a Pollyanna-ish notion, but I feel it in my heart.

I know there are hardened sexual criminals in this world, a few of whom are undoubtedly enrolled at USC, but I believe that most of the otherwise respectable college men who hurt women in this way do not fit that description. I suspect that most men who lure women to parties to get them drunk and have sex with them do not intend to ruin their lives; they merely intend to have a good time.

I am not being an apologist here. Their actions are immoral, despicable and criminal. I would punch any of them out if I had the chance. But often, I think, they are not malicious. They are participants in a date-rape culture that is frighteningly prevalent at USC and colleges across America, and they may not even think they're doing anything wrong. And that's the really scary thing.

In this day and age, virtually everyone, again excluding hardened sexual criminals, accepts that "no means no." Most would also agree that actual unconsciousness means no. And few would argue anymore—at least out loud—that a girl is "asking for it" simply because she is wearing a revealing dress or acting flirtatiously.

[Many college men] are participants in a date-rape culture that is frighteningly prevalent at . . . colleges across America.

But the lines are rarely so neatly drawn as that. And there is a whole culture of partying, drinking and sex that is fundamentally built around the ambiguities that arise when sex and alcohol mix.

Sure, it's wrong to use alcohol to coerce a girl—but what if you're merely cajoling her? What if you know she's drunk, but you're not sure how drunk? Does that give you a green light, or at least plausible deniability?

What if you're drunk, too? Does that mean you can rape her with a clear conscience? (Hint: If you're sober enough to ask yourself this question, the answer is no.)

What if you think she wants it—she never said so when she was sober, and you wouldn't bet your life on it, but you think so? It's OK then, right?

Only a sober "yes" means yes

Men who buy into this sort of logic—and there are many who do, to varying degrees—are looking at the definition of date rape as a technicality instead of a moral absolute. They are focusing not on doing the right thing, but on giving themselves cover. They wonder, "Can I get away with it?" or, "Can I justify it?" when they should be asking themselves, "Am I sure she'll be OK with this in the morning?"

I do not mean to vilify all men when I say this. How could I? I am a man. I know there are plenty of good men out there; I'd like to think that I'm one of them. Nor do I mean to say that parties are always bad or that alcohol is inherently evil.

But far too often, our half of the species lets our libido get the better of us, and we make the conscious choice to do things with a semi-conscious girl that we know she will, or might, wish had never happened.

"But women are fickle!" some men will protest. "It's not my fault if she wants it now and regrets it tomorrow!" That's not the point. Consensual trysts between sober adults of sound mind are not at issue here. It's when the sobriety and soundness of mind disappear that the problems begin.

Men . . . are in the best position to change things, to dismantle the date-rape culture.

We already know that "no means no," so let's add a few new rules to the rulebook: Possibly means no. Maybe means no. Probably means no. And if she's so drunk that she can't even give you a straight answer, that definitely means no.

Only a clear, sober "yes" means yes. If there is any doubt whatsoever, it isn't worth the risk. There will be other chances to get laid. The girl whose life you might ruin doesn't have another life.

These rules are based on two simple premises: chivalry and human decency. Unless both are entirely dead, we should be ensuring that the females in our lives are comfortable and happy—which, obviously, makes it a big no-no to do anything that would actually cause them harm. And make no mistake: any form, any degree of sexual assault causes women great harm.

Needed: a few good men

This is a key point. Somewhere along the way, some of us seem to have forgotten that we are supposed to treat women right, even if it requires a measure of self-sacrifice. Sure, you wanted it, and sure, you might have thought she wanted it, but did you think about the consequences if it turns out you were wrong? Your moral justification won't make her feel any better if she finds herself unable to trust anyone again for years. Why did you risk it?

The vast majority of participants in events like Take Back the Night are invariably female, and understandably so. The vast majority of college-age victims of sexual violence are women. But with all due respect to the many hard-working female activists who have made so much progress during the last 30 years in the battle against sexual violence, what the fight needs most now is a few good men.

Men, as the most frequent perpetrators of sexual violence, are in the best position to change things, to dismantle the date-rape culture. We need to speak out against it among our friends, to fight it in our own lives, to both practice and preach a values system that respects women and despises all forms of sexual assault.

Sexual violence is an ugly blot on the reputation of the male half of the human race, and it's up to us to clean up our gender's act.

12

Date Rape May Never Be Eradicated

Elizabeth Wurtzel

Elizabeth Wurtzel is the author of several books exploring women's issues, including Prozac Nation *and* Bitch: In Praise of Difficult Women, *from which this viewpoint was selected.*

Some women enjoy rough sexual activity and fantasize about being raped and beaten by men. These feelings do not indicate that most women want to be physically abused; rather, they demonstrate that sex contains dark impulses that may inexplicably flare up in heterosexual relationships. Contemporary feminism is concerned with eradicating these dark impulses by instituting dating codes such as "no means no," but sex is inherently dangerous. The mixed messages women give off during dating rituals are no excuse for date rape, but women should understand that flirtation and a few drinks can turn suddenly violent.

In an *Esquire* column from 1972, reprinted in her collection *Crazy Salad,* Nora Ephron admits to "this dreadful unliberated sex fantasy," one so ugly she can't share it with her consciousness-raising group (ah, the seventies) or even with her readers, except to say, "It has largely to do with being dominated by faceless males who rip my clothes off. That's just about all they have to do. Stare at me in this faceless way, go mad with desire, and rip my clothes off. It's terrific. In my sex fantasy, nobody ever loves me for my mind." Ms. Ephron doesn't elaborate much on this, though she does suggest that some harsher and rougher rape and battery follows all this ocular objectification. At any rate, I think it is a safe categorical rule—like the five years you add on to the given age of any woman over fifty, or the ten pounds you add on to the admitted weight of any woman at all—that whatever sexual fantasies someone is willing to divulge amount to maybe a tenth in degree of debauchery of what they really dream up. The only thing that we know for sure is that most of us have reveries about rape from one or another perspective, and almost none of us act on them (I shudder to think what actual rapists fantasize about).

Violent fantasies

And it's a funny thing about sexual fantasies of all kinds: unlike other types of fantasies—those flights of fancy about winning the lottery or showing the town bully who's boss or rescuing your dream girl from a car wreck—which we would love, without reservation, to experience in reality, most people really would not like their sexual desires fulfilled. It's not just that a man who wins the *Penthouse* sweepstakes and is granted command of a harem will learn the hard (and sore and not so hard) way that making love to twenty women at once is more exhausting than enjoyable—it's that most men don't even *want* to test-drive this daydream in the first place. And most women do not wish to be raped, maimed, bruised, choked, whipped or battered. But that doesn't mean the thought does not make them hot and soft and wet.

You see, many of us like a little bit of violence, or the fierce and fearsome possibilities implied by a domineering man whose touch is less than tender. Plenty of us have had some unnerving and unexpected sexual encounters where we've been hit, thrown on the floor, pushed against a wall, held down or shaken up, and many of us have found ourselves on all fours or thrown across some man's lap getting spanked like a bad, bad schoolgirl who is made to feel even naughtier as something warm shoots up between her thighs, as a tense ticklish quiver coruscates deep inside of her. The majority of us who've had such experiences can enjoy feeling dirty and debased and interested in what was happening, because despite date-rape hysteria and domestic violence media saturation, we ultimately have some sense that nothing too bad is *going* to happen. Somewhere in the apocrypha of the social compact, it is decreed that a *spanking* does not translate into a *beating*.

Feminism [will never] . . . snuff all the dark stuff out of sex.

But I know this is slippery logic. If we condone this little bit of brute force from men—and by definition, by asking them to just be men and be different from women, we kind of do—should we not consider it part of our opportunity costs in dealing with these creatures that it will sometimes get ugly, that it will occasionally get real? If only feminism or any other philosophy or moral code could come up with something so luscious that it could conquer these base impulses that fuel heterosexual love. If only it could outsmart the will to power, he with his strength, she with her sexual snare, and both with the rape fantasy—sublimated into the push-and-pull, the resistance-yield-conquest of common courtship—that is almost a necessity in every romantic relationship, for it is only in the saying no and playing hard to get that the tease and tension and titillation is born, even for healthy people. If feminism could snuff all the dark stuff out of sex and we could all just enjoy the edenic love that has the family-entertainment feel of a trip to Disney World, then sexism will be completely eradicated. But not until then.

So it's basically never.

Mixed messages, fine lines

And that's why there is a part of me that understands why Mike Tyson or members of the Dallas Cowboys assume that if a woman comes up to their hotel room late at night, it's because she means to stay awhile. And it doesn't mean that she's crashing on the couch. Or that she'll stay for tea and crumpets, clean her hands in a finger bowl of rose water, put her white gloves back on and then go home. It's not that it ought to be assumed that a woman who joins a man in his suite at the Ritz-Carlton after 11 P.M. is there to get laid, but if you happen to be dealing with pre-verbal professional athletes, it's a good idea to be careful. And be prepared. And, quite frankly, before you make the trip up the elevator to one of the top-floor rooms with VIP services like delivery of *The Wall Street Journal* each morning, it might be a good idea to be willing. Because late at night, in hotel beds with their cold, crisp sheets, in front of hotel TVs with their six choices of Spectravision, what people like to do is fuck. And who can blame them?

No does not *always mean no. It does, often enough, mean:* I'm not easy, try a little harder.

I believe Mike Tyson committed rape on that fateful beauty-pageant night in Indianapolis, and I am glad he was convicted and incarcerated for it. But I also think Desiree Washington was an idiot to be alone with Mike Tyson in *any* room with readily available horizontal surfaces—especially a hotel, whose utilitarian value is infused with sexy implications—if she wasn't wanting to get down and dirty. Because that's what people do. And because no *does not* always mean no. It does, often enough, mean: *I'm not easy, try a little harder*, or: *I want to but don't think I'm a slut*, or: *I really do want to, but I'm uncomfortable with the enormity of my sexual desires, so only if you force me will I be able to ignore my guilt.* Now, for the sake of the law, a line must be drawn, and no must mean *no*. But the mixed messages, not just in that little two-letter word but in all the rites of dating, will not be decoded and destroyed until we raise a generation of infants in perfectly appointed little Skinner boxes so that their brains are programmed from the earliest point to enjoy clean, utopian sex, the kind we had before the serpent, before we partook of the fruit of the Tree of the Knowledge of Good and Evil and opened our eyes and saw that we were naked and felt the shame which begot suspicion which pervaded everything. And bad as this was supposed to be—the Fall, the one with a capital letter—my guess is that before that day it was all procreational sex, it was mating season activity, it was animal—and by *animal* I mean bunny rabbits, not felines. But once we tasted forbidden fruit—from the *only* tree in the whole Garden of Eden that had been proscribed—we were given the gift of vision, and instead of seeing light, we discovered darkness.

And we thought it was good.

Now here we are: All these years later, and no one is exactly running to yank the string and get the lightbulb back on.

Still, no one wants to be date-raped and no one wants to be physically abused. But it is such a thin, fine line. When a rape or beating occurs between a man and woman who have just met—whether at a beauty pageant, a bar or a bar mitzvah—it's tough enough to make sense of how flirtation and a few drinks turned to aggravated assault. But with married couples, with longtime boyfriends and girlfriends: the mind boggles. A friend of mine, who is now an attorney, spent a couple of years between college and law school working for Linda Fairstein, head of the sex crimes unit at the Manhattan district attorney's office. My friend's entire job was interviewing women who had filed rape charges—these were cases where the situation was not desperate, the lines not so clear, no one was in the hospital—just to make sure that they hadn't then had sex the next night with the same guy voluntarily, or they had not since married him—or if, in fact, the woman's decision to go to the police to report the crime was not, in the first place, part of an escalating destructive dynamic the couple functioned in. When Pam talked to me about the women she dealt with, she never seemed to doubt the sincerity of their claims—she was quite sure *something* very bad must have happened; but there seemed to be real frustration with how the situation changed from minute to minute, how in a single conversation both the objective recall of events and the subjective interpretation of their meaning could vary wildly, how substance abuse blurred behavior, how love or what passed for it had the power to mess everything until it was beyond the limits of the law.

13

Colleges Should Punish Date Rapists with Shame Sanctions

Katharine K. Baker

Katharine K. Baker is an assistant professor of law at Chicago-Kent College of Law.

College administrative bodies charged with punishing convicted date rapists should use shame sanctions as an alternative to suspensions and expulsions. This form of punishment would require the rapist to wear a badge indicating that he had been found guilty of raping another student and would preclude him from participation in extracurricular activities. Singled out as a disgrace before the entire student body, the offender would readily understand that his behavior had deeply offended community norms. Potential rapists might also think twice before bringing similar scorn upon themselves. Because millions of people attend college in the United States, instituting shame sanctions for rapists will reformulate the rules of sexual interaction and begin a large-scale assault on date rape by curtailing macho behavior.

M ost college student victims of date rape, if they choose to come forward at all, seek redress from university disciplinary procedures, not from the criminal courts. One prominent date rape researcher has concluded that "most victims of acquaintance rape and sexual assault do not even attempt to have the assailant arrested; but they would like him to know that what he did was wrong."

For shame

Grass roots efforts by women on various college campuses in the early 1990s compelled universities to develop procedures for dealing with sexual assault. Federal law now requires colleges and universities to draft sexual assault policies and conduct disciplinary hearings. These hearings are usually not designed to replicate criminal court procedures. They involve less rigid standards of proof and relaxed evidentiary rules. They often do not require unanimity to reach a conviction. The composition of college adjudicative bodies varies depending on the school, but the proceedings are usually confidential and any rendered punishment usually involves some restriction on the perpetrator's access to the benefits of the university. In egregious cases this means expulsion. Usually, it means some lesser form of suspension, probation or dormitory restriction. The schools often try to keep the punishment, like the hearings themselves, confidential. . . . Although college tribunals should continue, as they by law must, to adjudicate cases of sexual aggression, they should re-think their punishments. Public sanctions designed not only to punish but to teach and steer social influence will be more effective than either banishing punishments used by universities now, or imprisonment, the traditional sanction used by the criminal law. College tribunals that can punish behavior that is wrongful if not criminally illegal, and can convict, without permanently branding, a date rapist, should be more willing to penalize date rapist behavior. Punishing date rapists with the alternative sanctions suggested here will help undermine the social institutions that currently encourage the offensive behavior. . . .

Changing the meaning through sanctions

In relatively close-knit communities, like college campuses, in which prestige and esteem play a critical role in people's daily lives, we may be able to use alternative sanctions as a way of de-coupling sexual conquest from masculinity. Suppose, for instance, that if a college tribunal or administrative body found that someone had committed date rape, he did not go to jail or leave campus for a semester or two. Instead, the perpetrator stayed on campus and for a period of time, a semester or a year, and was required to wear a bright orange armband or badge that was unmistakably associated with his sanction. His insignia would have to list his group associations, fraternity letters, sports team—all the affiliations that are normally listed beneath one's name in a college yearbook—so that he was bringing shame not only to himself but to his peer group. His picture, with his badge prominently displayed, should be published on a monthly or weekly basis in the school newspaper. He should also be barred from partaking in any extracurricular activities, sports teams, clubs, and fraternity organizations, through which students usually garner the esteem of their colleagues. The university could also forbid him to consume alcohol, a proscription that they could enforce through unannounced (and demeaning) urine tests. While he was being sanctioned, the date rapist would be in the community without being able to be an active part of it. For this period of time he would be stripped of all of the traditional means of acquiring masculine esteem. After completing his sentence, however, his penance would be over and he should be allowed to re-integrate himself into the community. Some re-integration is crucial. If the punished one loses hope of being able to rejoin the community, he will simply leave and join a subculture that accepts his behavior.

Apologies could also play an important role in sanctioning date rapists. For instance, the date rapist could be required to publicly apologize and acknowledge his weakness. Similarly, he could be required to explain publicly, in classrooms perhaps, what he did, why he did it, and how he now sees it as wrong. The perpetrator would not have to admit criminal wrongdoing, but he would have to admit wrongdoing. The class would not be allowed to jeer; they would have to listen, but he would have to explain why he was sorry. The rapist should have to acknowledge publicly that his behavior was morally wrong and worthy of scorn. He might also be asked to deliver to his victim, every day or every week, reparations of some kind. This act would force the rapist to focus on what all too many of these men fail to see, namely, the person who is hurt when they selfishly use sex to enhance their own esteem.

The past success of sanctions

Controlled efforts like this to shape social norms and change social meaning have worked in the past. Consider the following examples. In the eighteenth and nineteenth century, dueling—the act of retiring to a field and firing pistols at each other—was an important means of satisfying social insults between members of the elite classes. If one felt insulted, one challenged someone to a duel, and if one was challenged to a duel, one was compelled to fight or his honor would be damaged in the community. State governments were not particularly fond of this means of dispute resolution because it was remarkably arbitrary and left a considerable number of otherwise quite useful people dead. States tried to curtail the practice in a number of ways, including various unsuccessful attempts to simply outlaw dueling. Apparently, this strategy did not work because gentlemen placed the importance of their social honor above the importance of obeying the law. An anti-dueling strategy that arguably worked better was to forbid anyone who dueled from demonstrating their honor through another well-established practice, holding public office. This alternative sanction was effective because it directly addressed that which gave men the need, or incentive, to duel in the first place, i.e., their honor. By refusing to duel, gentlemen could argue that they were behaving honorably by maintaining their ability to hold office, not dishonorably by "wimping" out of the duel.

> *[The date rapist should be] required to wear a . . . badge that [is] unmistakably associated with his sanction.*

A similar strategy could work for rape. Currently, our policy for attacking rape mimics the attempts to outlaw dueling and it is just as ineffective. Young men place the importance of their masculinity above the importance of obeying the law, just as duelers placed the importance of their honor above the importance of obeying the law. If young men continue to preference their masculinity in this way, they will continue to break the law, particularly because breaking the law may be seen as another means of proving one's masculinity. However, if breaking this particular law was punished such that one's masculinity, like a Southern gentleman's honor, could not stay intact after one was caught, these young men might begin to worry more about their transgressions. If not only the individual, but his entire peer group, risked public humiliation, there might soon be strong peer pressure to avoid this risky behavior.

By using demeaning sanctions, like public display, communities can destabilize the link between sexual conquest and masculinity.

Alternative sanctions may be able to ambiguate both the meaning of nonconsensual sex and the meaning of stopping short of rape. By using demeaning sanctions, like public display, communities can destabilize the link between sexual conquest and masculinity. Instead of enhancing the perpetrator's masculinity, taking sex without consent could result in an emasculation of the perpetrator. In addition, stopping short of rape could suggest that one's masculinity and the status of one's peer group were important enough to forego the risk of a demeaning display. Instead of being seen as a "wimp," the man who does not join in the sexual exploits could be seen as the man more capable of valuing masculinity, honor and peer affiliation. The criminal law has tried to change the social meaning of date rape by tying it to other forms of rape. By minimizing the force and violence requirements and trying to define rape simply as nonconsensual sex, reform efforts implied that date rape is the equivalent of "real rape." From the perspective of the victim, tying date rape to more violent forms of rape and stranger rape makes eminently good sense. The feelings of fear, anger, shame, and impaired trust are comparable among victims of all types of rape. From the standpoint of rape reform, however, this tying strategy may have backfired because most men and many women view rape along a complex spectrum of permissibility. Because the line between date rape and consensual sex is so hard to draw, while the line between "real rape" and consensual sex is easy to draw, people refuse to accept that date rape is real rape, that X really is like Y. Y involves a man, probably a stranger jumping out of the dark with a weapon. For many, date rape just cannot be tied to those circumstances. Instead of tying, therefore, it may be worth trying to ambiguate. Instead of just saying X means Y, we may need to suggest that X also means Z. Z is demeaning and pathetic and inconsistent with the esteem traditionally associated with X. If X can mean Z, as well as Y, X becomes much more confusing and much less appealing. . . .

[Another] example involves drunk driving. Formerly, driving home after too many beers was seen as a macho and appropriate thing to do. One certainly did not ask someone else to drive or leave one's car and take a cab. Indeed, among men, asking someone else to drive home would have been very emasculating. Drunk people may have believed that they were doing something wrong by driving drunk, but that wrong was merely a violation of a technical rule for which the police could pull them over. The technical wrong had no meaningful purpose or consequence. Mothers Against Drunk Driving and similar groups began to alter people's drinking and driving behavior patterns by changing the crime of drunk driving from an essentially victimless act of bravado, to an act with potentially deadly consequences for very real victims.

Date rape, in the eyes of many date rapists and in the eyes of many jurors, is also still seen as a victimless crime. Thus, date rapists view themselves and are viewed by others as technical criminals, but not real criminals. If these men were forced to apologize for what they did, if they were forced to articulate how rape carelessly used women, they might begin to think twice about their actions, just as most people now think twice before having another beer when they have to drive home. Apologizing forces people to admit their wrongdoing in a way that criminal punishments often do not. It also forces people to appreciate the consequence of their actions and focus on whether the consequences are worth it.

A public acknowledgment of wrongdoing

The nontraditional nature of these sanctions should not be viewed as calls for mercy or attempts to impose mandatory mediation. Mercy involves mitigating a punishment that is otherwise deserved or meting out a punishment that is less than retribution or deterrence requires. Mercy has its place, but the public display and apology alternatives suggested here will not be particularly merciful. They will not "season justice" as mercy does. They will do justice by clearly negating whatever benefit the rapist gained from his act. . . . The suggested sanctions are also particularly retributive and likely to deter because they make the perpetrator subject to the same kind of public humiliation that rape victims suffer and they take away the esteem that motivated him to rape.

[Shame] sanctions take what has been treated as a largely private harm and transform it into an issue that demands community-wide response.

The victim will also always retain the right to ask the state to bring criminal charges. The victim should not be forced to forgive the perpetrator nor should she be forced to interact with him if she does not want to. The victim and the offender will not necessarily come to terms with each other; rather, the offender will have to come to terms with his behavior, in the context of a community that scorns that behavior. The sanctions proposed here, in contradistinction to Victim-Offender Mediation programs, do not make what had been considered a crime against the public into a private dispute that the parties work out amongst themselves. Rather, the proposed sanctions take what has been treated as a largely private harm and transform it into an issue that demands community-wide response.

Experts who study date rape and work with college age populations agree on the paramount need to sever sexually predatory behavior from notions of masculinity. The proposed sanctions try to do just that. Nonetheless, we must be careful in our attempts to manipulate notions of masculinity, lest we legitimate the status system that our culture already reads into gender. The most effective way to emasculate a perpetrator would probably be to make him expressly female—to make him wear women's lingerie or clothing. Yet punishing someone by feminizing him in this manner would trade on the misogynistic messages in our system of gender. For most people concerned with rape reform, this is an unequivocally unacceptable message for any punishment to send. Emasculation must therefore be achieved more indirectly. The sanctions suggested here emasculate indirectly by temporarily prohibiting men from displaying the masculine qualities of independence, pride, control and righteousness and requiring them to acknowledge publicly their dependence, humility, limitation and wrongdoing. The key is to make date rapists feel sorry for what they did and make others uninterested in emulating their behavior.

Why shame should work

By manipulating the punishments imposed on rapists, communities can help change the social meaning of rape by altering the context in which rapist behavior is evaluated. However, we must recognize that the shaming sanctions suggested here are a potentially dangerous means of trying to affect social change. In her article on the meaning and potential ramifications of shame sanctions ["The Meanings of Shame: Implications for Legal Reform," *Psychology, Public Policy & Law*, 1997], Toni Massaro highlights the importance of distinguishing between shame, shaming, and the shameful. Shame is a noun, an emotion; shaming is a verb, an external action; and to label something shameful is to make a normative judgment on a particular behavior or action. One can feel shame without having been a target of shaming. Shaming someone does not necessarily make them feel shame; nor does it necessarily lead to a shared understanding of what is shameful. "The chances that these [shaming] signals will be read and reinforced by others in a uniform fashion will depend on social proximity, norm cohesion and other highly contextual variables." . . . Notwithstanding these concerns, the proposed shaming sanctions should effectively curb date rape in college communities.

Punishing date rape with shame sanctions serves four goals. First, it sends an unequivocal message of public condemnation that will help people internalize the wrong of date rape. Second, it generally deters the population of potential date rapists by making them afraid of being emasculated. Third, it specifically deters individuals who will feel particularly diminished by the public display. Fourth, by including the perpetrator's group affiliations in the public display, alternative sanctions may retard, if not reverse, the peer pressure that currently encourages date rape.

Social disapproval that jeopardizes a man's masculine status will deter those most likely to rape.

First, as discussed above, prosecutors have difficulty securing date rape convictions because there is no clear moral consensus that date rape is wrong. Rapists see themselves as technical criminals not real criminals. Shaming sanctions will help solidify public consensus on the immorality of the act by sending an obvious public message of moral condemnation.

Rape will cease to be seen as a technical violation. As James Whitman argues, "it is simply wrong to suppose that the shaming state is not a maker of public norms." Because there is no clear norm condemning date rape, we need a maker of public norms.

Communities must shore up the norm against date rape not because, as is often the case with norm violations that inspire shame sanctions, our culture has experienced some kind of moral decline with regard to the normative proscription on date rape, but because the normative proscription on date rape has never existed. This is an area in which social norms currently do not "police the behavior better than any legal rule could." There is no clear social norm against date rape. "Public shaming generalizes familiar principles to unfamiliar or new contexts. It integrates new categories of wrongdoing . . . into pre-existing moral frameworks."

Moreover, the communal, public nature of shame sanctions is likely to do a better job of engendering a community-wide reaction than can more external, atomized criminal punishments or banishments, particularly in communities like college campuses, where "meaningful social connections . . . tend to make communities cohesive and their members emotionally vulnerable to social sanctions." Shame sanctions may not create cohesion or connection, but they are likely to be uniformly interpreted in communities that already have some of those qualities. Thus, they will likely send a clear message of moral condemnation.

Fear of emasculation

Second, because shame sanctions will be linked publicly to the motivation that inspires rapist behavior, that is, because they will be linked to the masculinity norm, they will deter men who are concerned about their masculinity. The potential date rapist who would rape to enhance his masculinity will be particularly afraid of emasculating shame sanctions. Massaro writes that "the threat of . . . shaming best deters the people who most fear social disapproval, who are usually not offenders." Date rapists do fear social disapproval, particularly with regard to their masculinity, but they have yet to have to encounter disapproval when they commit date rape. People fail to find the rapist's act problematic or they blame the victim for its occurrence. It is society's failure to communicate disapproval rather than the date rapist's failure to respond to disapproval that enables date rape. Clear, well communicated social disapproval that jeopardizes a man's masculine status will deter those most likely to rape.

Traditional criminal sanctions are supposed to create comparable kinds of deterrent effects, but criminal trials and punishments, which often take place outside of the immediate community in which the incident took place permit observers to establish distance. This distance allows third parties to view the criminals as social deviants and thus dismiss what they do not see. If forced to confront the consequences of date rape daily, members of the community will be less able to distance themselves from the rapist and his behavior. Characterizing the date rapist as pathological is precisely what reformers should avoid because it diverts attention from the extent to which the raping behavior is encouraged by social norms, and it allows other men who are likely to fall victim to the same masculinity norm, to view the rapist as more demonic that he actually is.

One way to minimize the degree to which the community demonizes the shamed rapist is to forbid public taunting. Although subject to some First Amendment concerns, this kind of regulation could take the form of many contemporary Hate Speech codes. Indeed, the purpose of the anti-taunting and Hate Speech codes are similar: to prevent any accentuation of ostracism or difference. Ironically, and perhaps hypocritically, the purpose of a public shaming ritual is to make the punished person isolated, publicly visible and different. The ultimate effectiveness of the sanction, on the other hand, depends on not making him too isolated or too demonic. If he feels completely isolated, he will leave the community. If the community sees him as too demonic, others will not recognize how prone they are to the same offending behavior. As John Brathwaite notes, however, there is "something to be said for hypocrisy." Surely there is nothing more hypocritical in the isolating/integrationist approach to shaming than there is in the current regime in which we criminalize behavior that we then refuse to punish. Integrative public sanctions that allow for some degree of re-integration offer a means of punishing without pathologizing. In doing so, they force a community to understand the offending behavior as its own creation.

If the date rapist's peer groups are publicized and indirectly shamed along with the rapist, the peer groups will have an incentive to re-evaluate the benefits of [macho behavior].

Third, the proposed sanctions will specifically deter the shamed rapist. Carl Schneider writes [in *Shame Exposure, and Privacy*] that "we experience shame when we feel we are placed out of the context within which we wish to be interpreted." Shame sanctions will place men who are very, very eager to demonstrate their masculinity, in public positions in which they are seen, by everyone, as humbled and diminished. They will feel shame. They may also feel other emotions, like anger or guilt, but they are likely also to feel shame because of the "special kind of visibility and exposure [from *Shame and the Self* by Francis J. Broucek]." Brathwaite explains [in *Crime, Shame, and Reintegration*], that "individuals are more susceptible to shaming by other individuals when they are in relationships of interdependency."

College campuses: well-suited to shame sanctions

College campuses offer a rare opportunity to use shame sanctions in an interdependent environment. Students are dependent on their peers for social status and on their universities for educational credentials. Universities and peer groups are, in turn, dependent on student populations for their members. Universities and peer groups also gain and lose status based on the achievements and actions of their members. University campuses are also communities in which there are repeated social interactions with the same people, another prerequisite for effective shame sanctions. Moreover, the relative homogeneity of college campuses helps ensure that the sanctions' message will be uniformly applied. One of the problems with shame sanctions in more diverse societies is that the very rich and the very poor can escape a sense of scorn either because their wealth can insulate them or because their poverty makes them impervious to social stigma. Thus as Massaro writes, shaming sanctions are most likely to specifically deter the "least dangerous offenders, that is, status conscious, shame-sensitive offenders such as middle class, first time offenders." College student date rapists fit that description almost perfectly.

Even if the [use of shame sanctions primarily] occurs on college campuses . . . it is important because it begins an effort to . . . reformulate rules of sexual interaction.

Nonetheless, Massaro warns [in "The Meaning of Shame"], shame sanctions imposed on the population most susceptible to their message may be the "most destructive, both to the offender and to the offender's family or other intimates who may suffer spillover effects of the offender's public humiliation." In the date rape context, however, this spillover effect is positive not negative. Indeed, it is because the offender's peer group is likely to suffer from these sanctions that the sanctions are likely to be effective.

If the date rapist's peer groups are publicized and indirectly shamed along with the rapist, the peer groups will have an incentive to re-evaluate the benefits of the frequent sex norm. If, as was suggested, peer groups currently bestow esteem based on the frequency of one's sexual encounters and pay little heed to the consensual nature of those encounters, the imposition of shame sanctions may create strong incentives to change that normative structure. The bestowal of esteem by peer groups may be inevitable and the masculinity norm may be intractable, but that does not mean that groups cannot start encouraging new, less risky systems of bestowing esteem for masculinity. Thus the fourth reason why shame sanctions should be effective: peer groups damaged by the spillover effects of shame are likely to develop new, less dangerous esteem systems. The power and influence of the frequent sex norm should diminish over time.

Admittedly, shame sanctions will be an especially harsh form of punishment for the date rapist because his yearning for social approval and his insecurity about his masculinity which give rise to his tendency to rape in the first place will make being the subject of a humbling public display particularly painful for him. Emasculating someone who places a high premium on masculinity is grave punishment indeed. It may, in fact, be humiliating. This is dangerous because as Avishai Marasalit explains [in *The Decent Society*], once punishment becomes humiliation it "rejects human beings as human." Without a sense of his own humanity, a shamed individual ceases to feel the connection to human society that makes him susceptible to social norms in the first place.

To reject shame sanctions because of the risk of humiliation associated with emasculization, however, concedes that impugning someone's masculinity necessarily impugns his human dignity. If the perpetrator feels and is perceived by others to have lost all human dignity because his gender identity is damaged, then it is clear we have come to believe that to be human is to be gendered. However empirically true this may seem, it is a deeply troubling conclusion for those who find gender norms restrictive, and it is a conclusion that suggests that we would rather incur the costs (to women, of rape) associated with overaccentuating gender than the costs (to men, of humiliation) associated with de-emphasizing gender.

In sum, the need to send an official message of condemnation, the likelihood that others will be deterred by shaming, the high probability that the offender will feel shame, and the benefits of the spillover effect all suggest that the proposed sanctions may be a just and effective means of trying to curb the prevalence of rape. They may also be an effective way to de-emphasize gender. . . .

Broader implications

The world is much bigger, of course, than the sum of its university campuses and there are many, many date rapes that happen in communities unable to use the kind of sanctions explored in this viewpoint. The under-inclusiveness of the remedy does not rob it of its influence, however. Over fifteen million people attend college in this country and countless others are related to those that do. The sample size effected by these remedies may not include everyone in this country, but it includes a sizable number. Moreover, the people who are affected are likely to be those in the best position to help shape social norms elsewhere. People who go to college are less likely to be a part of subcultures that shun social norms and they are more likely to be esteemed members of their communities. As such, they are more likely to be able to be what Cass Sunstein calls "norm entrepreneurs [in "Social Norms and Social Roles," *Columbia Law Review*, 1996]." Norms do not always change from the top down, but if a desire for esteem helps explain the existence of norms, people with esteem are in the best position to be able to affect norms. If alternative sanctions can help change the sexual norms of today's undergraduate population, there is likely to be a normative ripple effect of considerable magnitude.

Furthermore, college campuses do not exist in a vacuum. The press reports on what happens on college campuses. Consider the recent coverage of political correctness debates, sexual harassment and hate speech codes on college campuses. There is every reason to believe that the press will publicize these incidents.

In certain situations, the type of sanctions proposed here may also be appropriate for criminal convictions. Shaming critic Toni Massaro even concedes that criminal shaming may work "in proper contexts, through proper methods, and subject to appropriate limits." If a criminal court judge can identify a young, status-hungry man who has raped more out of carelessness and a desire for esteem than out of anger or venality, and that man has a discernible desire and need to be a part of a community that can shame him, substituting public display for imprisonment may be worthwhile.

Even if the brunt of the norm alteration occurs on college campuses as a result of administrative decisions, however, it is important because it begins an effort to emasculate sexually aggressive behavior and reformulate rules of sexual interaction. If the risk to college men of using sex to enhance their own esteem is a risk to their masculinity, men's tendency to view sex as a masculine privilege and biological inevitability will likely decrease. The less people view sex as a masculine privilege and biological imperative, the easier it is to view it as a process or a medium for communication through which the ultimate goal is mutual enjoyment or intimacy. Once sex is viewed as a fundamentally mutual assertive experience, nonconsensual sex ceases to represent some form of fungible alternative to consensual sex, and is seen as something truly "other." It will be easy to condemn the date rapist when nonconsensual sex is viewed as something truly "other," like having sex with a four year old.

If communities are to stop rapist behavior, they must reach out to the rapists themselves and those most likely to encourage the raping activity. The goal is not simply to label date rapist behavior as "other," but make people understand why it is "other." It is "other" because it hurts people. It is "other" because it is not about mutual pleasure and intimacy, but about selfish pursuit of one's own goals at the expense of another person's autonomy. It is "other" because it really is wrong. Because it is wrong, we must strive to make it about something other than masculinity.

14

Colleges Need Better Policies to Assist Date-Rape Victims

Heather M. Karjane, Bonnie S. Fisher, and Francis T. Cullen

Heather M. Karjane is the director of health and human development programs at the Education Development Center, a nonprofit research organization in Newton, Massachusetts. Bonnie S. Fisher and Francis T. Cullen are professors of criminal justice at the University of Cincinnati in Ohio.

Since one-in-five female college students are likely to suffer rape or attempted rape, American colleges must ensure that their sexual misconduct policies encourage rape victims to report assaults to authorities and give victims more control over the adjudication process. To support this effort, a Model Sexual Assault Policy Manual should be developed that colleges could adopt as a template for formulating better policies. In addition, programs that have proven to be effective in assisting victims of sexual assault should be recognized and shared among college faculties. Policies which inhibit victims from reporting assaults and identifying rape as a crime must be studied and eliminated.

The impetus for student-victim-oriented Congressional legislation throughout the 1990s, such as the *Clery Act*[1] was to ensure that institutions of higher education (IHEs) employ strategies to prevent and respond to reports of sexual assault on campus in a proactive manner and to provide current and prospective students and their parents with an accurate idea of the level of violence on campuses. Both national studies and smaller-scale research have consistently found that one in five female students suffer rape and/or rape attempts during their college years, most frequently at the hands of their peers. As such, prevention, response, and reporting policies should be built on definitions of sexual assault that

---

1. The Clery Act is a 1998 amendment to the 1990 Student Right-to-Know and Campus Security Act, which requires colleges to publicly disclose their crime statistics and security procedures on campus.

Heather M. Karjane, Bonnie S. Fisher, and Francis T. Cullen, *Campus Sexual Assault: How America's Institutions of Higher Education Respond*. Newton, MA: Education Development Center, Inc., 2002. Copyright © 2002 by Education Development Center. Reproduced by permission.

make it clear that this crime is most frequently committed by people known to the victim.

Underreported victimization

A key issue confronted by postsecondary institutions is that the vast majority of students who experience sexual assaults—on and off campus—do not report them to campus or law enforcement officials. The reasons for not reporting victimizations . . . are complex and unlikely to be fully overcome. The college community is affected by this underreporting in at least two significant ways. First, victims of sexual assault are unlikely to secure the counseling and support they need to cope with and heal from this potentially traumatic event in their lives making it more probable that they will engage in "self-blame," self-medication (e.g., disordered eating and excessive drinking) and other self-destructive behaviors. The friends they disclose their experience to are also likely to be affected, having their own feelings of anger, fear, and/or helplessness. In this way, one sexual assault can have a ripple effect. Second, unless sexual assaults are reported, students who sexually assault their classmates will not be subjected to appropriate sanctions and counseling. The possibility that they will continue to victimize others is thus increased.

Based on this research, we offer two types of recommendations: those aimed at providing support to IHEs and in creating comprehensive sexual assault policies that are specific to their school type, and those that suggest areas in need of further examination.

Design policies and protocols that prioritize victims' needs

Protocols for reporting sexual assault and rape should first consider the needs of victims themselves in terms of their healing process. A couple of strategies are suggested.

First, response and reporting policies should be designed to allow victims as much decision-making authority in the process as possible. Victims fear losing control over the reporting and adjudication processes, which is a barrier to their coming forth and making the initial reports. Policies should be designed to allow victims to make the decision about moving forward, stopping, or slowing down the pace at each juncture of the disclosure, reporting, and adjudication process. Explicit information regarding the policy and its different components—and the decisions to be made at each juncture—should be provided to the victim to inform her or his decisions. Also, victims should be informed of how each junction in the process effects their confidentiality.

Second, adjudication hearings should be fair. Victims of campus crime often seek acknowledgment of and justice for their experience; they seek respect within the campus system. One way to ensure that respect is to provide campus adjudication hearings that are fair to both parties. Operational rules and responsibilities should be explicit, unbiased, communicated to both parties, and adhered to. Current litigation instigated by students found responsible for sexual misconduct often centers on due process rights not being consistently applied. As these suits threaten the validity of the board's determination of responsibility, the needs of student victims are also compromised.

Third, response and reporting policies and policy materials should be gender-neutral and refer to the person who has experienced an assault as a "survivor," the term used by many victims of sexual assault in an effort to reclaim their lives. This term connotes the strength of living through and beyond the traumatic experience as opposed to focusing on the implied weakness in not being able to adequately protect oneself. Response policies should provide strategies to empower victims, rather than revictimize them by taking choices away or withholding information.

Fourth, protocols and policies should be widely distributed, written in lay terms, and explicitly supported by administration so that all students are aware of their rights and options before they need the system.

Develop a model sexual assault policy manual and education pamphlet

After analyzing the materials schools provided on their sexual assault policies, we came to three conclusions. First, many institutions either did not have such policies or could not provide them to us. Second, many institutions that had policies had them scattered about various documents, rather than in one easily accessible document. Third, only a few institutions had well-developed sexual assault policy statements that adequately defined sexual assault, listed services available to victims, clearly specified how victims could report an assault, and demarcated in detail the disciplinary process and procedures that would be used when a complaint of sexual assault was made. Four-year public and private nonprofit institutions, and, to a lesser extent, two-year public institutions and historically black colleges and universities (HBCUs), tended to have more complete policy statements. Even here, however, there was considerable variation in the clarity and thoroughness of the sexual assault policies.

[College] response and reporting policies should be designed to allow [rape] victims as much decision-making authority in the process as possible.

In this context, a major recommendation of this viewpoint is that an effort be made to develop a Model Sexual Assault Policy Manual that would provide separate prototypes for several types of institution: traditional four-year public or private non-residential and residential institutions, two-year non-residential public or private schools, and less-than-two-year institutions. These prototypes would provide schools with a template for developing sexual assault policies that make sense given the varying specifications of campus types. Although individual institutions may wish to add features to their policies, a model manual would provide clear guidance on "state of the art" practices in this area and for their school type. A model manual would assist the institutions that do not have the personnel or expertise to design an effective policy manual of their own; it would also mean that not every institution would have to "reinvent the wheel."

Once this *Model Sexual Assault Policy Manual* were developed, it could be placed on the Internet so that schools could download and modify it, as needed. Focus groups of college and university personnel involved in preventing and responding to sexual assaults—and especially students—could be used as part of the development of the model manual. This document could ultimately be an evolving manual that would be assessed and revised as its use became more prevalent in the United States.

In short, it is unlikely that responsible systematic sexual assault policies will be implemented across America's diverse postsecondary institutions without these institutions being given concrete guidance. The proposed *Model Sexual Assault Policy Manual* is one step—albeit a potentially salient step—in this direction.

The bewildering array of policies and procedures—many of which are buried in institutional documents that are hard to interpret and gain access to—make it unlikely that many students are well-informed about the sexual assault policies at their institutions. To help overcome this problem, we recommend that a pamphlet—perhaps called "Educating Students About Sexual Assault: What Is It? What to Do?"—be developed. Ideally, this pamphlet would be tied to the *Model Sexual Assault Policy Manual*, so that its guidance about sexual assault was consistent with its institution's policies and practices.

A model [sexual assault policy] manual would provide clear guidance on "state of the art" practices in [campus rape reporting and adjudication].

Regardless, even a general pamphlet would be useful in helping to instruct students about the nature of the sexual assaults that occur on- and off-campus and about what to do when a sexual assault occurs. Existing pamphlets at institutions would form a starting point for the development of an educational document that would have applicability nationwide.

In this document, special attention should be paid not only to victims of sexual assault but also to students to whom victims disclose their sexual victimization. As discussed, friends are most often the people that victims confide in when they are sexually assaulted. At present, there is little information for students, on how to assist friends who disclose a sexual assault.

Finally, this model educational pamphlet should be placed on the Internet, perhaps as part of a more comprehensive Web site on campus sexual victimization.

Develop a set of model services for victims and guidelines for reporting sexual offenses

Most institutions provide access to services—either on campus or within the local community—to students who have been victimized. Still, the extent and nature of these services differs markedly across and within types of institutions. These services are furthermore highly dependent on the type of IHE. For example, while a dedicated sexual assault response coordinator may be very useful within a large residential university setting, this type of response would be nonsensical at a small, non-residential campus. It would be useful, therefore, to develop a set of "model services" or "best practices" that have been shown empirically to assist victims of sexual assault as appropriate for different school types. Descriptions of these programs could be developed and made available both in document form and on the Internet.

A set of "model services" or "best practices" that have [proven] . . . to assist victims of sexual assault [should] be developed.

Further research is recommended to ensure evidence-based decision making with regard to effective programming. As such, effective prevention efforts, response policies and practices, facilitators to reporting, and adjudication practices should be investigated.

There is much confusion among the nation's IHEs regarding the exact data the *Clery Act* seeks to capture in annual security reports (ASRs) [filed by colleges to comply with the *Clery Act*]. We recommend that a formalized classification system with explicit definitions of sexual offenses, definitions of "campus," etc. be developed. Again, this classification system could be placed on the Internet—perhaps as part of a more comprehensive Web site on campus sexual victimization.

Our investigation suggests that the quality of the ASR data is dependent on the specific campus personnel required to submit data for the report. Similarly, IHE's reliance on particular types of campus security and/or law enforcement also appears to affect reporting, reporting policies, and student utilization of law enforcement and/or legal services. These issues need further examination.

Also needed is a systematic approach to collecting data on the use of "date rape drugs" such as Rohypnol, as identified in this research. This issue too warrants further scientific attention before policies and laws are developed to address it.

Evaluate policies which inhibit the victim's ability to report and identify rape as a crime

Campus administrators and rape trauma professionals offered opinions regarding their perceptions of particular policies and practices they felt functioned as barriers and facilitators to reporting in this research. Policies identified through survey and field research should be formally investigated. For instance, does offering an anonymous reporting option increase reporting as it is perceived to? Does it increase the use of the school's sexual assault response services?

Regrettably, the present research included only a limited victim perspective in terms of the data that was collected and analyzed. (Few victims were willing to come forward and be interviewed during site visits to colleges, although a few interviews with student victims were conducted.) Victims' perspective is greatly necessary and needs to be incorporated into the evaluation of reporting policies and practices.

The perspectives of the general population of students similarly need to be investigated, particularly as they relate to the filing of third-party reports of campus sexual assault. As underreporting by victims themselves is a significant obstacle to obtaining accurate statistics on campus, the use of third party reports can be extremely useful.

Underreporting by victims is a substantial problem with many contributory factors that need to be understood and addressed. As discussed, in order for a victim of a sexual assault to come forward and report the crime, she or he first has to identify that the experience that they have lived through is a crime worthy of a report to campus and local law enforcement authorities. Factors which have been noted in the research literature to contribute to a victim's ability to identify the experience they lived through as a criminal felony include: the adoption of stranger-rape myths [the false assumption that rape is typically committed by strangers], the relationship of the victim to their assailant, the use of alcohol before the assault, and the responses victims receive when they initially disclose their (traumatic yet possibly unnamed) experience to friends. More investigation of these and other contributory factors is needed to inform education and prevention programs aimed at students; this research should amply include students and student victims.

Investigate ethnic and other cultural factors in campus sexual assault

Little is known about the role of ethnic and other cultural differences in the area of campus sexual assault. National-level research using general population samples has reported that prevalence rape, forms of rape suffered, and post-assault consequences differ significantly among ethnic groups. As such, the questions arise as to whether or not these patterns are operative within college campuses. Effective prevention strategies, particularly for HBCUs and Native American tribal schools, are contingent on this currently limited knowledge. Furthermore, research as to the rates and experiences of lesbian, bisexual and transgendered women is virtually absent. Our final recommendation is that much-needed research effort be applied to investigation of ethnic, sexuality, and other cultural differences regarding sexual assault and reporting policies, and the issue of underreporting among student victims.

15

Campus Sexual Misconduct Hearings Are Flawed

Dorothy Rabinowitz

Dorothy Rabinowitz is a member of the Wall Street Journal's *editorial board and contributes articles to the paper's editorial page, from which this viewpoint was chosen. In 2001, she won the Pulitzer Prize in Commentary for her articles on American culture and society.*

A male college student is charged by a woman he briefly dated with having committed an act of unwanted sex. The college's investigation of the accusation is flawed from the outset, and an impartial hearing board returns a conviction, suspending the accused for three months and branding him a rapist in the eyes of his peers. This episode demonstrates how those accused of sexual misconduct rarely receive a fair hearing in university justice systems—the accuser's credibility is not questioned, and there are no judges asking if administrators have bothered to speak with the accused.

In the spring of 1996, a university official asked 20-year-old Brandeis junior David Schaer to come to her office. His presence would be helpful, the associate director of the Office of Student Life informed Mr. Schaer, because a student he had briefly dated on and off was upset, and needed support. Perhaps he could just come and listen to her.

Charged with unwanted sex

He was more than willing, aware as he was that a sexual encounter with the woman a few weeks earlier had gone awry, leaving them both discomfited. What he did not know, as he entered the Student Life office, was that he was already the subject of a charge the woman had just filed with the Brandeis police—that he had, in the delicate phrasing adopted by the university, committed an act of unwanted sex—and that anything he said at this meeting would figure in future testimony against him. Indeed, he was the only one of the three people entering that meeting who was unaware of his actual situation, for as it turned out, Alwina Bennett,

the Student Life official who had requested that Mr. Schaer come and listen to his friend, had herself escorted the woman to the Brandeis police.

When the three met in her office, Ms. Bennett suggested the woman
ask Mr. Schaer why he thought he was there. It was a query he would
have cause to remember.

"I think you feel I took advantage of a friend," David Schaer replied,
well aware of their conversation the day after, of the woman's dismay and
her hostile tone, of his own heated response that he had done everything
she told him to do—stopped when she said stop, continued when she
said go.

By the time the office meeting ended, he had learned of the police
complaint and also that the woman held him responsible for the perilous
emotional straits in which she found herself—for trouble she had sleeping, focusing and doing her schoolwork. She told him that his offense
against her was the first thing she thought about each morning and the
last thing on her mind at night, according to the account provided by the
associate director of student life. "You knew because I was drunk," the
woman charged, "that I couldn't consent to have sex with you."

When the accusing woman had departed, a much-shaken David
Schaer asked if he could tell Ms. Bennett what had actually happened that
night. He had absorbed all the strictures about consent he had learned at
school, about the woman's right to set the boundaries and say stop at any
point—had not only absorbed them but embraced them. No, she did not
want to hear it, the associate director replied. "I am the complainant's
support here," she instructed Mr. Schaer, now near tears. He pressed her
with questions and asked again if he could tell her his side, the official recalled in her later deposition. Noting his emotional state, she suggested
he instead find somebody else to talk to. She knew of no men's support
groups, Mr. Schaer remembers being told, but she was certain he could
find one.

Finding a men's support group was not prime among his concerns as
he left the familiar halls of the Student Life building where he had worked
and earned a certain respect, as he thought. The son of a middle-class
family from Armonk, New York, the tall, robust-looking Mr. Schaer, a biology major, had been exceptionally taken with the life he found at Brandeis. Quite simply, he loved the school and felt a powerful connection to
it—one far greater than any of his campus friends felt, as an ironic former
classmate recalls. Two aspects of his life at Brandeis he valued above all—
his work in the freshman orientation program and his role as editorial
board member and photo editor of the campus newspaper.

*David Schaer asked if he could tell [the school
official] what had actually happened that night. . . .
She did not want to hear it.*

In the weeks to come, he would lose one and be threatened with the
loss of the other, and these would be, compared with everything else, the
least of his worries. None of this did he begin to grasp as he left the meeting, distraught, to talk to family members and friends. Neither could he

have imagined, now, the elaborate maze of charges, proceedings and hostilities ahead, all of which would end up in a case that reached Massachusetts' highest court.

An invitation to "fool around"

This was no ordinary he-said, she-said conflict, the kind common in charges of date rape, a term now shunned by many university officials who instead use the term "unwanted sex." However it was described—and a Massachusetts appeals court would have something to say about that—it was trouble, begun in the early hours of Valentine's Day, 1996. About how it began, there is no dispute. Following a party where she had a few drinks with friends, a group that did not include David Schaer, the complainant retired to her room. Somewhere around 11:30 P.M., she called him and asked him to come over. He was reluctant, Mr. Schaer attested, and she persistent in her request that he come over, so they could "fool around." He told her he would call back. In a second call to him, around 1:15, Mr. Schaer said the complainant told him she wanted him to come and sleep over—she would go down and unlock the door for him. He was to take his shoes off, so as not to wake her housemates.

[Earlier statements] would [later] be presented as an admission of guilt, and officially recorded as evidence against him.

Asked, in a later deposition, what was said in the calls to Mr. Schaer, his accuser said that she did not remember. She did, however, remember—under questioning by Mr. Schaer's attorney—the purpose of the first call and the plans she made with Mr. Schaer.

Q: "What was the purpose?"
A: "So we could fool around."
Q: "What do you mean by fool around?"
A: "I don't know."
Q: "Fool around sexually?"
A: "Yes."

And had she made another phone call to Mr. Schaer? Yes, was the answer. And what was the purpose of that call?

A: "To see where he was."
Q: "To find out whether he was coming over?"
A: "I don't remember."

On the February 14 in question, of course, the depositions and the courtrooms, the campus judicial procedures and the bitterness that flowed from it all lay far ahead. Mr. Schaer had felt a touch grim when he left the woman's room that morning, suspecting that he had been summoned there as a replacement for the man she was actually interested in, who was ignoring her. This was the reason, he was certain, for the sexual debacle that had just ended.

Their prior brief encounters, which consisted mainly of oral sex and one incomplete exercise in intercourse, had not been notably joyful either.

This night they began with oral sex, which she soon asked him to stop, as he did. Then vaginal intercourse, which she apparently found painful and told him to cease. Mr. Schaer attests that at this point he asked if she would like him to leave, but that she told him to stay—she didn't mean to drive him crazy. After some conversation he understood that she was brooding about Jeremy, the man who dropped her, and who was, she suspected, probably in his room with another woman. Mr. Schaer offered to call and see, and was soon able—after a chat with Jeremy—to provide the comforting news that he was alone. Her mood somewhat improved, she got up and fumbled around in her desk to get one of the condoms she kept there—a lubricated kind, he thought, unlike the sort he brought. Now came another, longer coupling that she asked him to stop because she wanted to perform oral sex on him. This time, Mr. Schaer says, he asked if he could continue a few moments and finish, and that her answer was yes, and he should hurry up.

In the complainant's future version of events, she knew of no phone calls to Jeremy, she had not obtained a condom from her desk, she told her visitor she wanted no sexual activity and she in fact had been asleep when she found him entering her.

The day after the episode she called Mr. Schaer to express her unhappiness, to say she didn't know how her clothes had come off, and that she didn't know what she was going to do. What she was going to do was to become clear enough five weeks later, with the filing of her complaint.

A hearing board returns a conviction

In April, a Brandeis hearing board composed of five students and two faculty members met to consider the complainant's accusation that Mr. Schaer had called and then visited her and engaged in unwanted sexual activity. At this hearing, to which the accused and accuser both brought witnesses, the consequences of the conversation at the Student Life office, to which he had been summoned to help a friend, soon became clear. The associate director, Ms. Bennett, testified—as witness for the accuser—that David said, in her presence, that he "took advantage of a friend." This would be presented as an admission of guilt, and officially recorded as evidence against him—notwithstanding Mr. Schaer's bitter reminder that he had said something quite different. Also among the accuser's witnesses was the Brandeis police officer who had taken the complaint. Sergeant Betty Tehan told the hearing board that the complainant "looked like a rape victim."

[After his conviction,] the university . . . dealt with [David Schaer] as an outcast.

The members of the hearing board went off to consult and returned with a conviction. As the associate dean of student affairs put it in a statement, this case was about the lack of respect for the complainant's "integrity and personal rights and physical abuse which endangered her welfare, and David's unwelcome sexual advances which had the effect of interfering unreasonably with the complainants's educational and living environment."

David Schaer, as a consequence, was to be punished with a three-month suspension—from the day of his last spring final through August, during which time he would be barred from campus and all activities. He was to be on probation for the remainder of his time at Brandeis, and to undergo counseling.

These sanctions were far from the ones envisioned by the accuser, who wanted David Schaer suspended for no less than three years, and to be forced to resign at once from all student organizations and activities. Passionate in her belief that Mr. Schaer had escaped the measure of punishment due him, she protested to the administrators. Ms. Bennett warned Dean of Student Affairs Rod Crafts that such a brief suspension would cause discomfort and angst in the women's community.

In the university justice system, there are no questions as to evidence of the accuser's credibility.

Mr. Schaer in the meantime became the target of vocal hostility from the accuser's supporters, directed by a leader of the Committee on Rape Education—demonstrators not inclined to the university's preferred language, or distinctions like "unwanted sex." "Rapist Go Home" read the signs confronting Mr. Schaer, around his living quarters and elsewhere. Petitions went around asking that he be made to leave the campus at once.

He was, the dean of student affairs now warned him, "damaged goods," and it would be better if he transferred to another school. If he did so in time—before the sanctions were officially handed down—nothing would go on his record.

For David Schaer, daily life at Brandeis was now, indeed, a gauntlet to be run, where fellow students ran up to tell him he was disgusting and to say he should leave. His circle of friends, men and women, stood by him, which helped, but it could not alter the fact that the university of which he had been so proud now dealt with him as an outcast.

Fighting the suspension

Still, he would not cast himself out. In June, his Massachusetts attorney, David M. Lipton, filed a seven-count suit in superior court, charging the university had failed to honor its own code and accord Mr. Schaer basic rights. He asked also for an injunction of the suspension. To allow the lifting of this suspension, Brandeis attorney Alan D. Rose told the court, would surely imperil young women—freshman and others—on the campus during the summer. This was an odd argument, given the brevity of the suspension and the fact that Brandeis was prepared to receive Mr. Schaer again in September. Harvey A. Silverglate, the Massachusetts attorney who filed an amicus [friend of the court] brief on Mr. Schaer's behalf, observed that in the current political arrangements on the campuses, a summer suspension is the penalty handed down for the innocent.

Rejected by the lower court, Mr. Schaer proceeded to an intermediate appeals court, where a three-judge panel ruled that he had indeed cause to proceed with a case against Brandeis University. Noting the language used to charge Mr. Schaer, the author of the opinion wrote, "Stripped of euphemism, Brandeis's complaint against Schaer was that he raped a fellow student." The university hearing panel had moreover allowed "irrelevant and inflammatory evidence," and failed to apply the clear and convincing evidence standard. No one interviewed Mr. Schaer before the proceedings, and the court found there was nothing in the record to show anyone had evaluated the accuser's credibility. Brandeis officials have refused all comment, though at least two expressed astonishment that Mr. Schaer would continue arguing his case.

Ten private colleges in the area filed briefs in support of Brandeis when that university appealed to the Supreme Judicial Court of Massachusetts. The colleges feared intrusion into their internal judicial proceedings, and worried that if the judgment should stand, they could be swamped with litigation commenced by students brought up before panels like the one that sat in judgment on Mr. Schaer. They had, indeed, reason for concern, considering the vast complex of offenses, sexual and other, on which university panels now sit in judgment—accusations of intimidation, "creating a hostile environment" and similar vague offenses. In the university justice system, there are no questions as to evidence of the accuser's credibility, no judges asking if the administrators have troubled to talk to the accused.

The colleges were relieved of their concerns in September, when the Supreme Judicial Court of Massachusetts ruled for Brandeis, declaring, among other findings, that the university need not adhere to normal due process standards, but could act in accord with its own standards of justice. The colleges had a close call—a 3–2 opinion.

In turn Mr. Schaer managed—after a final year in which he was regularly reviled as a rapist—to graduate from Brandeis with honors, to enter graduate school and to meet the woman who would become his fiancée. It had been, in all, an expensive education.

Organizations to Contact

The editors have compiled the following list of organizations concerned with the issues debated in this book. The descriptions are derived from materials provided by the organizations. All have publications or information available for interested readers. The list was compiled on the date of publication of the present volume; the information provided here may change. Be aware that many organizations may take several weeks or longer to respond to inquiries, so allow as much time as possible.

Campus Outreach Services, Inc. (COS)
PO Box 8307, Radnor, PA 19087
(610) 989-0651 • fax: (610) 989-0652
e-mail: askkatie@aol.com • website: www.campusoutreachservices.com

COS is a for-profit organization that conducts date-rape prevention programs at colleges and high schools across the country. The company was founded by date-rape survivor and activist Katie Koestner to educate young people about the harm that date rape continues to cause women. The COS website provides free access to articles discussing the effectiveness of antirape programs and policies.

Center for the Prevention of Sexual and Domestic Violence (CPSDV)
2400 N. 45th St., Suite 10, Seattle, WA 98103
(206) 634-1903 • fax: (206) 634-0115
e-mail: cpsdv@cpsdv.org • website: www.cpsdv.org

The CPSDV is an educational resource center that works with both religious and secular communities throughout the United States and Canada to address the issues of sexual abuse and domestic violence. The center offers workshops concerning sexual misconduct by clergy, spouse abuse, child sexual abuse, rape, and pornography. Materials available from the CPSDV include the quarterly newsletter *Working Together* and the books *Violence Against Women and Children, Sexual Violence: The Unmentionable Sin*, and *Love Does No Harm: Sexual Ethics for the Rest of Us*.

Center for Women Policy Studies (CWPS)
1211 Connecticut Ave. NW, Suite 312, Washington, DC 20036
(202) 872-1770 • fax: (202) 296-8962
e-mail: cwps@centerwomenpolicy.org • website: www.centerwomenpolicy.org

The CWPS is an independent feminist policy research and advocacy institution established in 1972. The center studies policies affecting the social, legal, health, and economic status of women. It publishes numerous reports on violence against women, including *Victims No More: Girls Fight Back Against Male Violence* and *Violence Against Women and Girls: Research and Data in Brief*.

Ifeminists
e-mail: info@ifeminists.com • website: www.ifeminists.com

Ifeminists, or individual feminists, is an online forum for women who believe that more women should accept personal responsibility for their decisions. The group respects viewpoints that do not always agree with the orthodoxy of politically correct feminism, and it dismisses the notion that the government knows what is best for women. Ifeminists publishes weekly editorials and numerous articles on its website that are skeptical of feminist research on date rape, sexual abuse, and other issues affecting women.

Independent Women's Forum (IWF)
PO Box 3058, Arlington, VA 22203-0058
(800) 224-6000 • fax: (703) 558-4994
e-mail: info@iwf.org • website: www.iwf.org

The IWF advocates the conservative values of personal responsibility and self-reliance among women. It presents commentary opposed to the feminist movement's influence on the legal, economic, and educational spheres of American society. The forum publishes the *Women's Quarterly,* the monthly *Ex Femina* newsletter, and *SheThinks,* a monthly magazine critical of the feminist movement on college campuses.

Ms. Foundation for Women
120 Wall St., 33rd Fl., New York, NY 10005
(212) 742-2300 • fax: (212) 742-1653
e-mail: info@ms.foundation.org • website: www.ms.foundation.org

The foundation provided the funding for researcher Mary Koss's widely cited 1985 study on the high incidence of date rape on college campuses, and it continues to conduct training and public education programs to protect the safety and health of women. The foundation's publications include the quarterly *Ms. Foundation* newsletter and numerous reports and pamphlets, including *In Our Own Image,* a report critical of the media's influence on young women, and *Beyond Surviving: Toward a Movement to Prevent Child Sexual Abuse.*

National Association of College and University Attorneys
1 Dupont Circle, Suite 620, Washington, DC 20036
(202) 833-8390 • fax: (202) 296-8379
e-mail: nacua@nacua.org • website: www.nacua.org

The association represents approximately fourteen hundred U.S. and Canadian colleges and universities in legal matters. It compiles and distributes legal decisions, opinions, and other writings and information on legal problems affecting colleges and universities. Publications include *Acquaintance Rape on Campus: A Model for Institutional Response* and *Crime on Campus.*

National Center on Addiction and Substance Abuse (CASA)
Columbia University, 633 Third Ave., 19th Fl., New York, NY 10017-6706
(212) 841-5200 • fax: (212) 956-8020
website: www.casacolumbia.org

CASA conducts research to understand and reduce the social cost of substance abuse. It publishes several reports investigating how substance abuse can lead to sexual assaults, including *Rethinking Rights of Passage: Substance Abuse on America's Campuses* and *Dangerous Liaisons: Substance Abuse and Sex.* The center also publishes the quarterly newsletter *CASA Inside.*

National Coalition of Free Men
PO Box 582023, Minneapolis, MN 55458-2023
(888) 223-1280
e-mail: ncfm@ncfm.org • website: website: www.ncfm.org

The coalition's members include men seeking "a fair and balanced perspective on gender issues." The organization promotes men's legal rights in matters such as false accusation of rape, sexual harassment, and sexual abuse. It conducts research, sponsors educational programs, maintains a database on men's issues, and publishes the bimonthly newsletter *Transitions* and the online monthly *NCFM Gazette*.

NOW Legal Defense and Education Fund
395 Hudson St., New York, NY 10014
(212) 925-6635 • fax: (212) 226-1066
e-mail: lir@nowldef.org • website: www.nowldef.org

The NOW Legal Defense and Education Fund is a branch of the National Organization for Women (NOW). It provides legal referrals and conducts research on a broad range of issues concerning women and the law. It offers a comprehensive list of publications, including testimony on sexual harassment, books, articles, reports, and briefs. The fund assembles legal resource kits pertaining to a variety of issues, including violence against women.

Office for Victims of Crime Resource Center
810 7th St. NW, Washington, DC 20531
(800) 627-6872
e-mail: askov@ojp.usdoj.gov • website: www.ojp.usdoj.gov/ovc

Established in 1983 by the U.S. Department of Justice's Office for Victims of Crime, the resource center is a primary source of information regarding victim-related issues. It answers questions using national and regional statistics, research findings, and a network of victim advocates and organizations. The center publishes numerous reports on sexual assault, including *Sexual Assault Victimization*.

Sex Information and Education Council of the U.S. (SIECUS)
130 W. 42nd St., Suite 350, New York, NY 10036-7802
(202) 819-9770 • fax: (212) 819-9776
e-mail: siecus@siecus.org • website: www.siecus.org

SIECUS is a clearinghouse for information on sexuality, with a special interest in sex education. It publishes sex education curricula, the bimonthly newsletter *SIECUS Report,* and fact sheets on sex education issues. Its articles, bibliographies, and book reviews often address the role of sex education in identifying, reducing, and preventing sexual violence.

Wellesley Centers for Women (WCW)
Wellesley College, 106 Central St., Wellesley, MA 02481
(781) 283-2500 • fax: (781) 283-2504
e-mail: wcw@wellesley.edu • website: www.wcwonline.org

The WCW is a liberal, profeminist community of scholars engaged in research and training efforts to improve the lives of women. It publishes the results of its numerous research projects, including the report *Sexual Harassment and Gender Violence in Schools*, which discusses date rape as a troubling issue affecting young women.

Bibliography

Books

Jeffrey R. Benedict	*Athletes and Acquaintance Rape.* Thousand Oaks, CA: Sage, 1998.
Raquel Kennedy Bergen, ed.	*Issues in Intimate Violence.* Thousand Oaks, CA: Sage, 1998.
Maria Bevacqua	*Rape on the Public Agenda: Feminism and the Politics of Sexual Assault.* Boston: Northeastern University Press, 2000.
Ann J. Cahill	*Rethinking Rape.* Ithaca, NY: Cornell University Press, 2001.
Mark Cowling	*Date Rape and Consent.* Aldershot, England: Ashgate, 1998.
Lisa M. Cuklanz	*Rape on Primetime.* Philadelphia: University of Pennsylvania Press, 1999.
Leslie Francis, ed.	*Date Rape: Feminism, Philosophy, and the Law.* University Park: Pennsylvania State University Press, 1996.
Pamela Haag	*Consent: Sexual Rights and the Transformation of American Liberalism.* Ithaca, NY: Cornell University Press, 1999.
Danielle Hain	*Date Rape: Unmixing Messages.* Tempe, AZ: Do It Now Foundation, 2000.
Ida M. Johnson and Robert T. Sigler	*Forced Sexual Intercourse in Intimate Relationships.* Aldershot, England: Dartmouth and Ashgate, 1997.
Sharon Lamb, ed.	*New Versions of Victims: Feminists Struggle with the Concept.* New York: New York University Press, 1999.
Scott Lindquist	*The Date Rape Prevention Book: The Essential Guide for Girls and Women.* Naperville, IL: Sourcebooks, 2000.
Wendy McElroy	*The Reasonable Woman: A Guide to Intellectual Survival.* Amherst, NY: Prometheus Books, 1998.
Andrea Parrot	*Coping with Date and Acquaintance Rape.* New York: Rosen, 1999.
Daphne Patai	*Heterophobia: Sexual Harassment and the Future of Feminism.* Lanham, MD: Rowman & Littlefield, 1998.
Lynn M. Phillips	*Flirting with Danger: Young Women's Reflections on Sexuality and Domination.* New York: New York University Press, 1999.
Katie Roiphe	*The Morning After: Sex, Fear, and Feminism on Campus.* New York: Little, Brown, 1994.

Peggy Reeves Sanday	*Women at the Center: Life in a Modern Matriarchy.* Ithaca, NY: Cornell University Press, 2002.
Francis Shuker-Haines	*Everything You Need to Know About Date Rape.* New York: Rosen, 1999.
Christina Hoff Sommers	*The War Against Boys: How Misguided Feminism Is Harming Our Young Men.* New York: Simon and Schuster, 2000.
Christina Hoff Sommers	*Who Stole Feminism? How Women Have Betrayed Women.* New York: Simon and Schuster, 1994.
U.S. Congress House Committee on Commerce Staff	*Date Rape Drugs.* Washington, DC: U.S. Government Printing Office, 1999.
Cathy Young	*Ceasefire! Why Women and Men Must Join Forces to Achieve True Equality.* New York: The Free Press, 1999.

Periodicals

Amy Argetsinger	"Campus Efforts to Prevent Rape Changing Focus," *Washington Post*, April 16, 2001.
Azell Murphy Cavaan	"Universities Struggle with Date-Rape Cases," *Boston Herald*, March 14, 1999.
Jodi S. Cohen	"Clinton Signs Date-Rape Law Sparked by Michigan Teen's Death," *Detroit News*, February 20, 2000.
Ruth G. Davis	"How to Talk Your Way Out of a Date Rape," *Cosmopolitan*, December 2000.
Eric Dexheimer	"Friend or Foe: In an Era of Hooking Up, When Does a Date Become Rape?" *Westword*, December 13, 2001.
Sandy Fertman	"Drugged and Raped," *Teen Magazine*, June 2001.
Nadja Burns Gould and Veronica Reed Ryback	"Misconceptions About Date Rape," *Boston Globe*, March 12, 1999.
Guardian	"The Price of Crying Rape," February 9, 2000.
Mark Hemingway	"Campus Justice Goes Ape," *American Spectator*, December 1, 2000.
Nat Hentoff	"Blind Justice on Morningside Heights," *Village Voice*, November 15–21, 2000.
Noelle Howey	"By Any Other Name," *Ms.*, February/March 2001.
Johanna Jainchill	"In Their Defense," *New York Times*, October 13, 2002.
Me Ra Koh	"My Boyfriend Raped Me," *Campus Life*, September 2001.
Donna Leinwand	"Use of 'Date Rape' Drug Surges," *USA Today*, January 28, 2002.
Jemima Mackee	"Who Was the Victim on the Campus?" *London Daily Telegraph*, July 11, 2002.

Wendy McElroy · "The New Mythology of Rape," June 26, 2001, www.ifeminists.com.

Karen Meyers · "It Takes Two to Stop Tragedy of Date Rape," *Los Angeles Times*, March 28, 1999.

Mary K. Moore and Leah Ginsberg · "The Date Rapist's Scary New Weapon," *Cosmopolitan*, February 1999.

Dennis O'Brien · "Experts Warn of Alcohol as Date-Rape Drug," *Baltimore Sun*, November 13, 2000.

Jaime Sneider · "Civil Liberties Go on Trial at Columbia University," *National Review*, March 7, 2001.

Onell R. Soto · "Drug-Assisted Date Rape on the Rise, Hard to Prosecute," *San Diego Union-Tribune*, June 3, 2001.

Marilyn Stasio · "It's Not Just a Women's Issue Anymore: On College Campuses Across the Country, Growing Numbers of Young Men Are Taking Responsibility for Sexual Violence," *Parade*, January 21, 2001.

Carie Windham · "Sexual Assault Becoming More Prevalent on College Campuses," *University Wire*, October 10, 2002.

Cathy Young · "A Turning Tide on Date Rape," *Boston Globe*, May 13, 2002.

Kate Zernike · "Campus Court at Harvard Alters Policy on Evidence," *New York Times*, May 9, 2002.

Index